Delia's
HAPPY CHRISTMAS

Delia's
HAPPY CHRISTMAS

A Christmas Wish

photography by Petrina Tinslay

EBURY
PRESS

CONTENTS

CHRISTMAS is a thoroughly good thing – something that Charles Dickens instinctively understood when he wrote his famous *Christmas Carol*. The main character, Ebenezer Scrooge, was a cynic who hated Christmas so much that he thought 'anyone with Merry Christmas on their lips should be boiled with his own pudding and buried with a stake of holly in his heart'.

The story of his conversion, and how he became an ardent lover of Christmas, is a perceptive and powerful observation on human life. Dickens understood the innate need we all have to step aside from the daily grind and take time out for feasting, sharing and having fun. With or without any specific religious belief Christmas fulfils that intrinsic human need for celebration. So as Dickens put it elsewhere 'draw up your chair nearer the blazing fire, fill your glass and send round the song'.

However there is always a practical side to all this in that someone will have to prepare the feast and at the same time share the celebrations. Therefore we hope that what follows is a practical and helpful collection of ideas, recipes and suggestions that will keep things on track and make that possible.

I first attempted this all of nineteen years ago, and the response and appreciation shown by countless Christmas cooks has been phenomenal. So why do it again? First, there is a whole new generation of those who have to cook Christmas for the first time. Secondly, the devoted followers of the original will, I'm sure, appreciate a brand new collection of recipes alongside the old ones.

We have included all the traditional recipes that have served people well over the years, and if I have an agenda myself this time round it would be to encourage younger people, who have never been shown that home-made traditional Christmas recipes – the puddings, the cakes, the mincemeat, and not least cooking the turkey itself – are not difficult if they are explained simply. So don't be afraid. A little help is all you need and, hopefully, it's right here.

There is an eclectic range of recipes, so there's much to choose from and, I hope, something to suit everyone. My last wish is, most of all, that you will have a very happy time preparing and cooking for Christmas, an even happier time enjoying the feast, and that (with or without the blazing fire) you will, as Dickens suggested, fill up your glasses and have a very Happy Christmas.

Delia Smith
Christmas 2009

Part 1
THE PLAN

HAPPINESS IS GETTING A GRIP EARLY
Make a plan

The wisdom that comes only late in life (in my case anyway) has taught me that Christmas is always going to arrive much sooner than I think. So, instead of playing mind games and being in denial, I have had to learn to face up to its imminence full-on. If you are the one who's doing Christmas you will have to do the same. It involves work, but work that's planned for with calm control becomes a pleasure instead of a pressure, and you don't end up in a heap on Christmas afternoon.

A HOME-MADE CHRISTMAS
Home-made anything is always going to (i) cost less, and (ii) be, oh, so much better. By my reckoning, if you settle down in mid-October with your diary you will need to mark off four full days (or the equivalent) for your Christmas preparations and – while you're relaxed – plan your menus.

Day One is for shopping: half a day shopping at home online or by mail order, and half a day in the shops. Day Two is for making the Christmas cake, pudding and mincemeat. Day Three is cooking for the freezer. Day Four will be your last-minute preparations before the big day itself.

It might seem like rather a lot of time to devote, but don't forget this will be a quieter time when you can stop for breaks or listen to the radio. I know all these things are available straight off the supermarket shelf but compare peaceful home cooking with the stress of the high street, the parking, the crowds, and it's a no-brainer.

HOME-MADE CUTS THE COST
There has always been the choice: save time or save money. But the 'cash-rich, time-poor' category so beloved of the consumer researchers could be a dying breed as the recession continues to roll on. So while there are certainly some last-minute suggestions in this book (see page 231) which would come straight off the supermarket shelves, for everything else there could never be a better time to save money. Home-made versions can be astonishingly cheaper: here are a few 2009 price comparisons.

A 150g portion of Traditional Christmas Pudding from this book costs 44p compared with similar helpings of good quality commercial puddings which cost from £1 to £2 and beyond.

A 100g slice of home-made Christmas cake (at 28p) costs a quarter of any superior supermarket brand (£1.10 at least, often more).

A single mince pie in the luxury class from a supermarket will cost you 38p or more. One from the recipe in this book will set you back just 9p.

If you get a grip early and make a plan, I believe you can save money and some sanity at the same time.

ARMCHAIR SHOPPING
Christmas delivered

What a revolution it has been, shopping online along with mail order. No parking the car, no checkout queues, no frantic searching of endless supermarket shelves. At Christmas, the biggest family feast in the calendar and a time for something special, it really comes into its own. It's a positive joy to have so many of the ingredients ordered in peace and calm, then delivered to your door. The following is a list of suppliers who have served us faithfully for years.

KELLY TURKEY FARMS A 6.3kg oven-ready bronze free-range turkey will serve eight with plenty for leftovers. Check on last delivery date. 01245 223581 *www.kellyturkeys.com*

PEELES Specialise in the wonderful Norfolk Black turkeys, which weigh in at 5–5.5kg. 01362 850237 *www.peelesblackturkeys.co.uk*

LANE FARM COUNTRY FOODS I always order a 2.25kg collar of bacon, plus 900g of pork sausagemeat for the stuffing and 225g of fat streaky bacon for the turkey. Check on last delivery date. 01379 384593 *www.lanefarm.co.uk*

ALEX SPINK & SONS To make the Arbroath Smokie Mousse (see page 100) or Souffléd Arbroath Smokie Creams with Foaming Hollandaise (see page 291). 01241 879056 *www.arbroathsmokiesonline.co.uk*

SPRINGS SMOKED SALMON We always treat ourselves to a side of smoked salmon to be eaten between Boxing Day and New Year's Day. 01903 815066 *www.springs-post.co.uk*

MATTHEW STEVENS AND SON Having fresh fish and shellfish delivered straight to you from the Cornish coast is a great time-saver now that local fishmongers are in short supply. 01736 799392 *www.mstevensandson.co.uk*

EMMETT'S STORES Specialise in the famous Suffolk Black hams, as well as Spanish ingredients including – the big bonus – Pedro Ximénez sherry (see Vanilla Bean Ice Cream with Raisins Soaked in Pedro Ximénez Sherry, page 245). 01728 660250 *www.emmettsham.co.uk*

GOODMAN'S GEESE For a beautiful, very high-quality, free-range goose that's oven-ready. 01299 896272 *www.goodmansgeese.co.uk*

FLETCHERS OF AUCHTERMUCHTY Suppliers of superb-quality venison, which arrives trimmed and ready to go. 01337 828369 *www.seriouslygoodvenison.co.uk*

AUBREY ALLEN Suppliers of guinea fowl, Gressingham duck and Blythburgh free-range pork. 01926 311208 *www.aubreyallen.co.uk*

DONALD RUSSELL Suppliers of beef, lamb, pork, poultry and game. 01467 629666 *www.donaldrussell.com*

FRATELLI CAMISA For all Italian products, including panettone and the best dried wild porcini, called Fruttibosco. 01992 763076 *www.camisa.co.uk*

LUIGI'S Another great online Italian deli, with particularly good antipasti and charcuterie; also chestnut flour and panettone. 020 3051 9352 *www.luigismailorder.com*

NEAL'S YARD DAIRY Renowned for their British cheeses. Personally I order their Strictly Traditional Christmas cheese box. 020 7500 7575 *www.nealsyarddairyshop.co.uk*

BOOKHAM FINE FOODS For a vegetarian version of Parmesan cheese. 01323 636110 *www.bookhams.com*

FORTNUM & MASON Wonderful chocolates, pâtés de fruit and – our favourites – Pruneaux d'Agen Fourrés, luscious prunes stuffed with prune purée to go with coffee and liqueurs. 0845 300 1707 *www.fortnumandmason.com*

CLEMENT FAUGIER For marrons glaces and crème de marron (sweetened chestnut purée) direct from France. Order from *www.clementfaugier.fr* (use the facility on your search engine to translate).

JANE ASHER PARTY CAKES AND SUGARCRAFT All things for cake decoration, including the shooting-star cookie cutter, sugar sparkles for the Chocolate & Sour Cherry Crumble (see page 214) and star sparklers for the Petits Monts Blancs (see page 205). 020 7584 6177 *www.janeasher.com*

For an extensive list of suppliers, see *deliaonline.com*

CHRISTMAS LASTS FOR 8 DAYS
Be prepared!

Well, it has kind of crept up on us over the years, and now become a sort of mini-holiday. My own philosophy about Christmas cooking is that most of it should be prepared in advance, so that for two or three of those days there's absolutely minimal cooking because you already have ham, turkey, mince pies, cake, cheese and all the rest.

Beyond that there may be a little more to do, but with some pre-planning and good use of the freezer and store cupboard, it's possible to cope comfortably with the extra days as well. For my part I don't want to go anywhere near a shop till after the New Year – and that in itself is a holiday for me!

The following is just a suggestion for how you could plan the 8 days. For instance, if you have your bacon (or gammon) on Christmas Eve you will have plenty left over to serve cold alongside slices of turkey, with pickles and chutneys. We always buy the wonderfully flavoured Fenland (dirty) celery: scrub, dry and prepare it, then wrap in large polythene bags. It will keep in the vegetable drawer of the fridge for most of the holiday, ready to serve with cheese.

Having a selection of cheeses, chutneys and pickles, smoked salmon, sausage rolls (in the freezer), mince pies (likewise) and Christmas cake means there is always an instant snack meal around. We also have some other treasures tucked away in the freezer as well (see page 21).

Here are suggested menus for the eight days – the first three being a ritual that is always followed in our house. Another must in our own plan is lunch at the local pub on one of the days, as it's essential to get out at least once and be served by others for a change.

CHRISTMAS DAY
EVENING

Only if you can!
Sausage rolls, pickled
shallots, turkey stuffing
(and bread sauce)
sandwiches, cold bacon and
sharp mustard sandwiches

BOXING DAY
SUPPER

Hand-sliced smoked salmon,
with Irish Soda Bread, capers
and cayenne pepper

.....

English cheeses with nuts,
muscatel raisins, Medjool dates
and celery,
served with port

CHRISTMAS EVE
SUPPER

Scallops in the Shell

.....

Roast Collar of Bacon (or
Gammon) with Blackened
Crackling *served with*
Cumberland Sauce
Jacket Potato Wedges with
Melting Cheese & Spring
Onion, Traditional Braised
Red Cabbage with Apples

.....

Cranberry Jellies with
Frosted Cranberries

CHRISTMAS DAY
LUNCH

Roast Bronze or Norfolk Black
Free-range Turkey with Pork,
Sage & Onion Stuffing
served with
roast potatoes, parsnips and
button sprouts
Giblet Gravy, Cranberry & Orange
Relish, Traditional Bread Sauce

.....

Traditional Christmas Pudding
with Christmas Rum Sauce

BOXING DAY
LUNCH

Cold cuts, slices of turkey
and collar of bacon (or gammon)
served with
Michael's Chunky Sauté Potatoes
in Turkey Dripping
Pickles, chutneys and cold sauces

.....

Traditional English Trifle
or warm Traditional Mince Pies

27 DECEMBER
LUNCH

Cold cuts served with
Brussels Bubble-and-Squeak
Pickles, chutneys
and cold sauces

.....

Christmas Cracker Puddings
with Mascarpone Rum
Cream

27 DECEMBER
SUPPER

Potted Pork or Venison,
or Pheasant Terrine
served with
various accompaniments and
lots of good bread

.....

Iced Chocolate Chestnut Torte

28 DECEMBER
LIGHT LUNCH

Smoked Salmon or Kipper Rarebit

.....

Warm Traditional Mince Pies

28 DECEMBER
SUPPER

Venison Braised in Guinness & Port
with Pickled Walnuts *served with*
mashed potato and celeriac

.....

Coconut & Lime Cheesecake with
a Confit of Limes

30 DECEMBER
LUNCH

Turkey Flan with Leeks & Cheese
served with
watercress salad
or Stilton Rarebit
or sliced smoked salmon

.....

Prune and Armagnac Ice Cream

30 DECEMBER
SUPPER

Pappardelle Pie with Wild
Mushrooms & Taleggio

.....

Chocolate & Sour Cherry
Crumble
served with
chilled pouring cream

NEW YEAR'S EVE
DINNER 2

Partan Bree

.....

Braised Venison with Bacon,
Chestnuts & Wild Mushrooms
in a Rich Madeira Sauce

.....

Scots Trifle with Drambuie

29 DECEMBER
LUNCH

English Colonial Curry with
Turkey and basmati rice
served with
poppadoms, mango
chutney and lime pickle

·····

Frozen Chocolate and Vanilla
Crème Brûlées

29 DECEMBER
SUPPER

A Very Special Seafood Risotto

·····

Panettone Bread & Butter Pudding
with Marsala

NEW YEAR'S EVE
DINNER 1

Souffléd Arbroath Smokie Creams
with Foaming Hollandaise

·····

Haggis Pie with Tatties & Neeps
& Whisky Sauce

·····

Cranachan with Caramelised
Oatmeal & Raspberry Sauce

DRINKS PARTY
MENU

Parma Ham, Pecorino &
Rosemary Crisps

·····

Blinis with Smoked Salmon
& Salmon Caviar

·····

Caviar Canapés

·····

Pistachio Sables

·····

Cheddar, Sage & Onion
'Sausage' Rolls

·····

Traditional Mince Pies

BUFFET
MENU

A Stilton & Lancashire Cheese
Terrine with Spiced Pear Confit

·····

Fillet of Beef in Pastry with
Horseradish, Crème Fraiche &
Mustard Sauce

·····

Tomato Tart with Swiss Cheese
& Rosemary

·····

A selection of salads (pages 90–93)

·····

Italian Chocolate Nut Christmas Cake
Panettone & Zabaglione Trifle

HOLIDAY ON ICE
The friendly store cupboard & well-stocked freezer

With the Christmas holiday now extended beyond a week, if you possibly can set aside a day in the run-up to the festival to stock the freezer, you will be so grateful when the time comes to be able to select tomorrow's menus (or at least part of them) before you go to bed each night. It means you, the cook, can enjoy the holiday alongside everyone else!

If you're like me, this will begin with the mother of all freezer clearouts to acquire some space (it's been long overdue anyway, hasn't it?). Below are some suggestions as to what can be made ahead and then frozen for up to one month.

FOR CHRISTMAS DAY
All stuffings
Custard for the trifle
Christmas Rum Sauce
Traditional Bread Sauce
Cranberry & Orange Relish
Cooked mince pies (45 minutes to defrost at room temperature)
Cooked sausage rolls (1 hour to defrost at room temperature)

SOUPS & STARTERS
All soups (except crab)
Pheasant Terrine
Potted Pork and Venison
Scallops in the Shell (can be cooked from frozen – see page 104)
Duck Liver Pâté with Armagnac

MAIN COURSES
Slow Braised Belly Pork with Bacon, Apples & Cider
Mustard Rabbit Braised in Cider
Venison Braised in Guinness & Port with Pickled Walnuts
Venison Sausages Braised in White Wine with Caramelised Chestnuts
Braised Venison with Bacon, Chestnuts & Wild Mushrooms in a Rich Madeira Sauce

Pot-roasted Pheasants in Madeira

VEGETARIAN CHRISTMAS
Macadamia & Pistachio Nut Roast
Tomato Tart with Swiss Cheese & Rosemary
Cheese & Parsnip Roulade with Sage & Onion Stuffing
Cheddar, Sage & Onion 'Sausage' Rolls

VEGETABLES IN WINTER
Traditional Braised Red Cabbage with Apples
Brussels Bubble-and-Squeak (before frying)
Purée of Potato & Celeriac with Garlic
Parsnips with Parmesan

SWEET DISHES
The Famous Chocolate Truffle Torte
Iced Chocolate Chestnut Torte
Frozen Chocolate & Vanilla Crème Brûlées
Coconut & Lime Cheesecake
Maple Walnut Cheesecake
Fallen Chocolate Soufflé with Armagnac Prunes
Chocolate Chestnut Log
All ice creams

OTHER OPTIONS
Bread sliced for sandwiches
Baguettes and bread rolls
Soda bread
Butter and milk
Frozen pastry cases
Pastry
Foaming Hollandaise

NOTE ON FROZEN TURKEY We advise buying a fresh turkey but if that's not possible don't forget to allow plenty of time to defrost slowly and completely. Allow up to 3 days in the fridge and remove the giblets as soon as it's thawed.

All defrosting is best done slowly in the fridge overnight unless we've suggested otherwise in the recipes.

JUST SO YOU WON'T FORGET...
Lists & more lists

Since the first Christmas book was published I have each year used the shopping lists in it and found them helpful as a starting point. It is impossible to list every ingredient in this list, but what is set out below are general lists that you can add to when you have decided what you are going to cook.

GENERAL STORE CUPBOARD

Flour
- [ ] Cornflour
- [ ] Plain
- [ ] Sauce
- [ ] Self-raising
- [ ] Strong

Nuts
- [ ] Almonds: whole skin-on and blanched, ground and toasted flaked
- [ ] Brazils, hazels, pecans and walnuts

Dried Fruits
- [ ] Apricots and prunes (no-soak)
- [ ] Cherries, glacé and dry sour
- [ ] Currants
- [ ] Glacé if using for decoration
- [ ] Raisins
- [ ] Sultanas
- [ ] Whole candied peel

Spices
- [ ] Cinnamon: sticks and ground
- [ ] Cloves: whole and ground
- [ ] Ginger: ground, preserved and crystallised
- [ ] Juniper berries
- [ ] Mace: blade and ground
- [ ] Mixed spice: ground
- [ ] Nutmeg: whole
- [ ] Salt and pepper

Sugar
- [ ] Glycerine
- [ ] Golden caster
- [ ] Granulated
- [ ] Icing
- [ ] Liquid glucose

Preserves
- [ ] Apricot jam
- [ ] Marmalade
- [ ] Redcurrant jelly

Baking powder
Cornichons
Crème de marrons (sweetened chestnut purée)
Dark chocolate (70–75% cocoa solids)
Dried yeast
English mustard: dry
Fine capers
Marigold Swiss Vegetable Bouillon
Marrons glacés
Oil: olive and groundnut
Porcini mushrooms: dried
Shredded suet
Vinegar: cider, red wine and white wine

FREEZER
Ice creams
Ice for drinks
Pastry
Peeled chestnuts: if not using vac-packed

ALCOHOL
Armagnac
Brandy
Calvados
Champagne or medium-dry sparkling white wine
Cider
Madeira: rich and Sercial dry
Marsala wine
Mixers
Pedro Ximénez sherry
Port
Rum
Sherry: medium and dry
Stout
Vermouth: dry
Wine
Red, full-bodied
Dry white

GENERAL NON-FOOD SHOPPING
Baking parchment
Batteries
Bin liners, freezer bags and plastic freezer boxes
Brown paper
Cake boards
Cake tins: 18cm square or 20cm round
Camera: memory cards, film and batteries
Clingfilm
Cocktail sticks
Decorative candles
Gift wrap, tape, tags and ties
Hangover remedy
Kitchen paper
Kitchen string
Long matches for flaming the pudding
Mince pie tins
Muslin
Napkins
Party crackers and streamers
Preserving jars
Pudding basin and small pudding basins
Roasting tin for turkey
Shooting-star cutter and silver balls
Silver or gold standard muffin cases
Spare light bulbs and fuses
Swiss roll tin (approx. 30 x 20cm)
Tree lights in working order
Turkey-width foil

WEEK BEFORE CHRISTMAS
Bacon, sausages and sausagemeat
Bread and rolls
Feuilles de brick (brick pastry)
Butter
Cheese and biscuits
Cranberries

Cream: whipping, double and single
Crème fraîche
Eggs
Fromage frais (8%)
Milk (including Channel Island)
Parmesan
Pastry: puff and shortcrust (if not making your own)
Peeled chestnuts: vac-packed if not using frozen
Tea, coffee, water and soft drinks
Trifle sponges
White bread for crumbs and croutons
Yoghurt

Now is the time to decide which turkey stuffing you intend to make and buy the appropriate ingredients

LAST-MINUTE FRUIT AND VEGETABLES
Apples: Bramley, Cox's and red
Bananas
Brussels sprouts
Carrots
Celery
Clementines
Medjool dates
Ginger root
Grapes
Leeks
Lemons
Limes
Onions, garlic and shallots
Oranges
Parsnips
Potatoes for roasting
Red cabbage
Salad
Spring onions
Watercress
Herbs: parsley, sage and thyme

A Christmas Wish

Part 2

THE RECIPES

All kinds of CHRISTMAS CAKES

YES, IT IS NOW possible to buy a Christmas cake, and there are some pretty good ones around. But, that said, a home-made one is in quite a different league. Not only is it better but it's surprisingly cheaper. It is also one of the most pleasurable advance preparations for Christmas. So take some time out in November – before the panic sets in – and fill the house with all the evocative aromas of Christmas home baking. Then tuck it away in a cupboard and each week 'feed' it by making small holes in the top and bottom with a cocktail stick and spoon in extra brandy or whatever you choose. (Note: lining papers for cake tins can be bought in packs from Lakeland and kitchen stores, and instructions on how to line tins are at deliaonline.com)

MY CLASSIC CHRISTMAS CAKE

'This, with no apologies, is a Christmas cake that has been in print for 21 years, has been made and loved by thousands and is, along with the Traditional Christmas Pudding [see page 46], *one of the most popular recipes I've produced.'* The above was the introduction to this recipe nineteen years ago and absolutely nothing has changed, except even more thousands have made it and loved it.

450g currants

175g sultanas

175g raisins

50g glacé cherries, rinsed, dried and finely chopped

50g whole candied peel, finely chopped

3 tablespoons brandy

225g plain flour

½ teaspoon salt

¼ teaspoon nutmeg, freshly grated

½ teaspoon ground mixed spice

225g unsalted butter

225g soft brown sugar

4 eggs

50g almonds, chopped (skin on is OK)

1 dessertspoon black treacle

the grated zest of 1 lemon

the grated zest of 1 orange

110g whole blanched almonds (only if you don't intend to ice the cake)

A 20cm round or an 18cm square tin, greased and lined with a double thickness of baking parchment. Tie a band of brown paper round the outside of the tin for extra protection.

You need to begin this cake the night before you want to bake it. All you do is weigh out the dried fruit and peel, place it in a mixing bowl and mix in the brandy as evenly and thoroughly as possible. Cover the bowl with a clean tea towel and leave the fruit to absorb the brandy for 12 hours.

Next day preheat the oven to 140°C/gas mark 1. Then measure out all the rest of the ingredients, ticking them off to make quite sure they're all there. The treacle will be easier to measure if you remove the lid and place the tin in a small pan of barely simmering water.

Now begin the cake by sifting the flour, salt and spices into a large mixing bowl, lifting the sieve up high to give the flour a good airing. Next, in a separate large mixing bowl, whisk the butter and sugar together until it's light, pale and fluffy.

Now beat the eggs in a separate bowl and add them to the creamed mixture a tablespoonful at a time; keep the whisk running until all the egg is incorporated. If you add the eggs slowly by degrees like this the mixture won't curdle. If it does, don't worry, any cake full of such beautiful things can't fail to taste good! When all the egg has been added, fold in the flour and spices using gentle, folding movements and not beating at all (this is to keep all that precious air in). Now fold in the fruit, peel, chopped nuts and treacle and finally the grated lemon and orange zests.

Next, using a large kitchen spoon, transfer the cake mixture into the prepared tin, spread it out evenly with the back of the spoon and, if you don't intend to ice the cake, lightly drop the whole blanched almonds in circles or squares all over the surface. Finally cover the top of the cake with a double square of baking parchment with a 50p-size hole in the centre (this gives extra protection during the long, slow cooking). Bake the cake on the lowest shelf of the oven for 4½–4¾ hours until it feels springy in the centre when lightly touched. Sometimes it can take up to ½–¾ hour longer than this, but in any case don't look for 4 hours.

Cool the cake for 30 minutes in the tin, then remove it to a wire rack to finish cooling. When it's cold, 'feed' it (see page 27), wrap it in double baking parchment secured with an elastic band and either wrap again in foil or store in an airtight tin. You can now feed it at odd intervals until you need to ice or eat it.

CREOLE CHRISTMAS CAKE

This recipe is for those who want a complete break with tradition and try something different. In the Caribbean where the sugar cane is grown recipes abound for something called 'Black Cake' and this is one particular version, which came from the wife of a plantation manager. I would describe it as being much more fruit than cake, and just to say don't be put off by the large amount of alcohol or the length of time the fruit is steeped in it. First, it's an incredibly easy cake to make, and secondly you'll love it so much you'll be glad to have all the booze tucked away ready for next year.

FOR THE PRE-SOAKING

3 tablespoons rum
3 tablespoons brandy
3 tablespoons cherry brandy
3 tablespoons port
3 tablespoons water
1½ teaspoons Angostura bitters
½ teaspoon ground cinnamon
½ teaspoon nutmeg, freshly grated
½ teaspoon ground cloves
½ teaspoon salt
1½ teaspoons pure vanilla extract
1 tablespoon molasses sugar
450g raisins
225g currants
110g no-soak prunes, chopped
50g glacé cherries, chopped
110g whole candied peel, finely
    chopped
50g mixed chopped nuts

FOR THE CAKE

250g self-raising flour
250g demerara sugar
250g butter, at room temperature
5 eggs

A 20cm square cake tin, greased,
    and the base and sides lined
    with a double thickness of baking
    parchment.

One week before you intend to bake the cake, measure out the rum, brandy, cherry brandy, port, water and bitters into a large saucepan. Then add the rest of the pre-soaking ingredients, ticking them with a pencil as you go to make sure nothing gets left out. Now stir and bring the mixture up to simmering point, then, keeping the heat low, simmer very gently for 15 minutes. After that allow everything to cool completely then pour the mixture into a large jar with a lid or an airtight plastic container and leave it in the fridge for 7 days, shaking or stirring it around from time to time.

When you are ready to bake the cake, preheat the oven to 140°C/gas mark 1. All you do is measure out the flour, sugar and softened butter into a very large mixing bowl, then add the eggs and either whisk or beat with a wooden spoon until everything is evenly blended. Now gradually fold in the fruit mixture until it's all evenly distributed. Then spoon the mixture into the prepared tin, levelling the surface with the back of the spoon.

Bake the cake in the centre of the oven for 3 hours without opening the door, then cover the cake with a double thickness of baking parchment and continue to bake it for a further hour or until the centre feels springy when lightly touched.

Cool the cake for 45 minutes in the tin, then remove it to a wire rack to finish cooling. When it's completely cold, wrap in double baking parchment and foil and store in an airtight tin or polythene box. Creole cake does improve with keeping for about 1 month before cutting. Feed it as in the previous recipe with even more booze at odd intervals (see page 27). The nut topping (on page 35) will work well for a decoration, or just a thin layer of Almond Icing (Marzipan) and icing on the top (see pages 35 and 32).

CHRISTMAS CAKE ICINGS & TOPPINGS

It has long been my conviction that Christmas is not the best time for creative cake decorations. I do realise that there are those whose lives are more organised than mine, who have Christmas all sewn up early and who can look forward to a leisurely period devoted to wielding a piping-bag and modelling paste. But for the rest of us pressured Christmas caterers I have devised the simplest, speediest Christmas cake decorations possible. Bearing in mind that in whatever shape the icing sugar and almond icing (marzipan) arrive on the cake they will always taste the same, the key to these suggestions of mine is that they will look classy with a minimum of effort. What has changed, though, is that it is now possible to buy good quality fondant and almond icing ready-made.

ROYAL ICING
FOR A ROUGH 'SNOW' SCENE FOR A 18CM SQUARE OR A 20CM ROUND ALMOND ICED CAKE

I confess this has often been for me a last-minute affair late on Christmas Eve. When I was a child there was a robin or Father Christmas handed down through generations to decorate with, but now a sprig of holly brushed with egg white and sprinkled with caster sugar in the centre of the cake will give a festive touch.

500g icing sugar, sifted
3 medium egg whites
1 teaspoon glycerine

Place the egg whites in a bowl and stir in the icing sugar, a spoonful at a time, until the icing falls thickly from the spoon. At this stage, stop adding any more sugar and whisk with an electric whisk for 10 minutes or until the icing stands up in stiff peaks, then stir in the glycerine.

Now spread the icing all over the top and sides of the cake as evenly as possible, using a palette knife. Switch to a broad-bladed knife (or smaller palette knife) to 'spike' the icing all over to give a snow-scene effect. Leave the cake overnight for the icing to dry out before placing it in a container till needed.

FONDANT ICING
FOR A 18CM SQUARE OR A 20CM ROUND ALMOND ICED CAKE

This is for those who like a softer icing but prefer to have a home-made version.

450g icing sugar, sifted
1 egg white, beaten
½ teaspoon pure vanilla extract
2 tablespoons liquid glucose
TO ROLL
2 tablespoons icing sugar
1 tablespoon cornflour

Begin by sifting the icing sugar into a medium bowl and making a well in the centre. Now put the egg white, vanilla and liquid glucose into the well and stir with a wooden spoon, gradually incorporating the icing sugar until it is too stiff to stir any more. Then, using your hands, form the icing into a ball before turning out onto a clean, smooth, dry surface and kneading for about 5 minutes until it becomes completely smooth (if the icing is sticky knead in a little more icing sugar, or if it is dry run a little cold water over your fingers).

Then roll out the icing onto a clean surface dusted with a mixture of icing sugar and cornflour, and keep giving it quarter turns between each roll. Once it is rolled to the right size cover the cake as soon as possible. If you want to make it ahead, it can be kept tightly wrapped in the fridge for 3 days (though once it is on the cake it does not need to be refrigerated).

GLAZED NUT TOPPING

This is suitable for all cakes and is good for people who don't like the extra sweetness of icing.

45 pecan nut halves
15 whole Brazil nuts
16 walnut halves
1 heaped tablespoon apricot jam
2 tablespoons brandy

First of all preheat the grill to the highest setting for 10 minutes and lightly toast the nuts, which not only gives them a better colour but a nicer flavour too. Be very careful though to watch them like a hawk: they really only need a couple of minutes if the grill is very hot and they should be pale gold rather than deep brown!

While they're cooling, place the apricot jam and brandy in a small saucepan and heat them gently together, whisking until they are thoroughly blended. Now, using a brush, paint some of the mixture all over the surface of the cake. Then arrange the nuts in whatever pattern you like. There's room for real artistic licence here, so if you're not that way inclined you could rope in someone else – this bit after all, does not involve cooking, just artistic talent. Finally, brush all the beautifully arranged nuts with lots more glaze, then store the cake in a tin or polythene box until it's needed.
NOTE For keeping-qualities, see Glacé Fruit Topping (page 36).

ALMOND ICING (MARZIPAN)
FOR A 18CM SQUARE OR A 20CM ROUND CAKE

Home-made almond icing is superior so I've included it here if you have time to make it, otherwise you can use ready-made.

350g ground almonds
175g icing sugar, plus extra for dusting
175g caster sugar
3 medium eggs, 1 of them separated
⅓ teaspoon pure almond extract
1 teaspoon lemon juice
1 teaspoon brandy

Begin by sifting the icing sugar and caster sugar into a large bowl, then stir in the whole eggs and the egg yolk. Place the bowl over a pan of barely simmering water and whisk for about 12 minutes, until the mixture is thick and fluffy. Then remove the bowl from the heat and sit the base in about 5cm of cold water. Whisk in the almond extract, lemon juice and brandy and continue to whisk until the mixture is cool. At this point stir in the ground almonds and knead to form a firm paste.

Now divide the paste by cutting off one-third of it. Dust a working surface with icing sugar and roll the smaller piece of paste to fit the top of the cake. Next brush the top of the cake all over with egg white, then turn it upside down and place it centrally on the rolled-out paste. Using a palette knife, press the edges of the paste up all round the edges of the cake, then turn the cake the right way up to deal with the sides.

Once again dust the working surface with icing sugar, and roll out the rest of the paste into an oblong 35 x 15cm. Divide this in half lengthways, then brush the sides of the cake with egg white and fix the two strips of almond paste all around the sides – you can smooth over the joins, first with a knife then with a rolling pin. Now leave the cake, covered with a clean cloth, for as long as possible up to 7 days.
NOTE If you wish to use ready-made almond icing (marzipan) you will need a 700g quantity to cover a 18cm square or a 20cm round cake as above.

GLACÉ FRUIT TOPPING
FOR A 18CM SQUARE OR A 20CM ROUND CAKE

At Christmas there are so many unusual glacé fruits available in the shops that seem to disappear at other times of the year. These can make very attractive alternative toppings for Christmas cakes. There are cherries (in all colours), glacé pineapples, peaches and I've even seen strawberries. You can, of course, use any combination you like. I personally like dark glossy prunes with the russet tones of figs and apricots. There really couldn't be an easier or quicker way to top a cake. Just finish it off by tying it with a pretty Christmas ribbon. One point to note: the amounts of the fruit are approximate, since this will ultimately depend on how artistic you may or may not be and how much you pile on.

8 no-soak prunes
6 no-soak apricot halves
2 no-soak figs, halved
5 glacé cherries (or any other combination of glacé fruits)
1 heaped tablespoon apricot jam
2 tablespoons brandy

First of all, heat the jam and the brandy together in a pan, whisking well until they are thoroughly blended. Then, using a brush, coat the surface of the cake quite generously with the mixture.

Next arrange the fruits in rows or circles on top of the cake, making as pretty a pattern as you can. Brush the fruits, again quite generously, with a coating of the glaze. Then cool the cake and store in a sealed container till needed. The brandy acts as a preservative and the topping will keep well (stored in a cool place) for several weeks. Don't worry about the keeping-quality of this glaze – we have stored glazed cakes for three months and they were still in beautiful condition.

SIMPLE DECORATION FOR A CHRISTMAS CAKE
FOR A 18CM SQUARE OR A 20CM ROUND CAKE

1 heaped tablespoon apricot jam
1 tablespoon Armagnac
350g ready-made almond icing (marzipan)
350g ready-to-roll white icing
a little icing sugar
a little beaten egg white
silver balls, to decorate

A shooting-star cookie cutter (available from Jane Asher Party Cakes and Sugarcraft, see page 15)

First melt the jam with the Armagnac in a small saucepan, stirring until all the lumps have dissolved. Now, using a brush, coat the surface of the cake quite generously. Take the almond icing (marzipan) and roll it out on a surface lightly dusted with icing sugar and cut out to fit the top of the cake. Then place this over the top of the cake.

Repeat with the icing and place this over the marzipan. Using the cutter, cut out a shooting star from the remaining rolled-out icing, dampen one side of it with cold water and place this side on top of the cake.

Decorate the edges of the cake and the star with silver balls, using a little beaten egg white mixed with a little icing sugar as a glue to keep the silver balls in place.

ITALIAN CHOCOLATE NUT CHRISTMAS CAKE

This recipe has been given to me by my favourite Italian cookery writer, Anna Del Conte, and is from her charming book *Amaretto, Apple Cake and Artichokes.* It can be served at tea-time or as a dessert. Either way it's great with whipped cream or vanilla ice cream.

225g dark chocolate (70-75% cocoa solids)

25g unsalted butter, melted and slightly cooled, plus a little extra for the tin

2 rounded tablespoons fine breadcrumbs

225g whole blanched hazelnuts

225g walnut pieces

5 drops pure vanilla extract

65ml brandy

1 teaspoon ground cinnamon

200g golden caster sugar

5 eggs, separated

1 large navel orange, scrubbed under warm water and the peel (without the pith) removed with a potato peeler and very finely chopped

A 20cm round, loose-bottomed cake tin.

Preheat the oven to 180°C/gas mark 4.

Begin by buttering the cake tin generously, then sprinkle the inside with the breadcrumbs, shaking off any excess. Put the hazelnuts and walnut pieces in a food processor, then break the chocolate into small pieces and add it to the nuts. Pulse the machine on and off until the mixture is of a grainy consistency but not finely ground. If you don't have a food processor, you can chop the ingredients by hand using a sharp knife.

Transfer the mixture to a large bowl and stir in the vanilla extract, brandy, cinnamon, melted butter and sugar, mixing thoroughly. Now gradually add the egg yolks, mixing them in very well, and, finally, add the orange peel. Next, whisk the egg whites to the stiff-peak stage, but not so thick that they become dry. Gently fold them into the chocolate mixture with a large metal spoon, a few tablespoons at a time, cutting through the mixture with a high movement to incorporate plenty of air.

When all the egg whites have been folded in, spoon the mixture into the prepared cake tin and bake in the oven on the centre shelf for about 1 hour to 1 hour 10 minutes. Cover the cake loosely with baking parchment for the last 10 minutes if it's becoming too brown.

The cake is ready when it feels springy in the centre when lightly touched. Then leave it to rest in the tin for a couple of minutes, before turning it out on to a wire rack to cool. Store in the fridge, wrapped in foil, and eat within 2 weeks. The cake will also freeze well, again wrapped in foil.

STOLLEN

At Christmas time in Austria they traditionally serve something called *stollen*: it is a rich, fruity yeast bread filled with almond icing (marzipan) and topped with a light glacé icing. If you have a number of people staying over the holiday, this is wonderful served warmed through at breakfast. If it is not all eaten when it's fresh, you can also lightly toast it in slices. In fact it is so good it's worth making two and freezing one (it freezes beautifully).

350g strong white bread flour

¼ teaspoon salt

2 teaspoons easy-blend yeast

50g caster sugar

150ml milk

110g softened butter

1 egg, beaten

40g currants

50g sultanas

40g no-soak dried apricots, chopped

40g dried sour cherries

25g whole candied peel, finely chopped

25g almonds, chopped

the grated zest of 1 lemon

175g white almond icing (marzipan)

FOR THE GLAZE

110g icing sugar, sifted

2 tablespoons lemon juice

A large baking sheet, lightly greased.

First sift 300g of the flour together with the salt into a mixing bowl. Sprinkle in the easy-blend yeast and sugar and give it all a stir before making a well in the centre. Pour in the milk, then add the softened butter and beaten egg. Mix everything together, either with your hands or with a wooden spoon – until the mixture is well blended and leaves the side of the bowl cleanly. Then work in the fruits, peel, nuts and lemon zest, distributing them as evenly as possible. Knead the dough on a work surface sprinkled with 25g of the remaining flour for 5 minutes, until it is springy and elastic.

Now leave the dough in the bowl in a warm place, covered with clingfilm, until it has doubled in size (the time this takes will vary depending on the temperature – it can be up to 2 hours). After that turn the risen dough out on to a board dusted with the remaining flour and knock the air out of it and knead until the dough is smooth and elastic. At this stage roll or press out the dough into an oblong 25 x 20cm. Using your hands, roll out the almond icing (marzipan) to form a sausage shape and place this along the centre of the dough, finishing just short of the edges.

Fold the dough over the marzipan and carefully place the whole thing on the baking sheet, allowing plenty of room for expansion. Leave it to prove in a warm place until it has doubled in size again. Preheat the oven to 190°C/gas mark 5, then bake in the oven for 35–40 minutes. Allow it to cool on the baking sheet for about 5 minutes before lifting it on to a wire rack to finish cooling.

Meanwhile make the glaze by mixing the sifted icing sugar with the lemon juice, then use a small palette knife to spread this all over the top surface of the stollen (while it is still warm). Serve as fresh as possible, cut into thick slices, with or without butter.

CHESTNUT CUPCAKES
MAKES 8

Since the craze for cupcakes has crept up on us, it seems appropriate to include a Christmas version which (along with the Italian Chocolate Nut Christmas Cake on page 38) will satisfy those who don't want or like fruit cake. The good thing here is 1 x tin of 250g crème de marrons is the exact amount needed.

150g crème de marrons (sweetened chestnut purée)
110g butter, very soft
2 eggs, beaten
110g chestnut flour (available at health food shops or see page 15)
1½ teaspoons baking powder
4 tablespoons milk

FOR THE TOPPING
100g crème de marrons
200g light mascarpone
3 marrons glacés, thinly sliced
1 rounded teaspoon icing sugar

Eight standard muffin cases and a deep bun tin measuring 35 x 26cm.

Preheat the oven to 170°C/gas mark 3.

First place the butter and the 150g of crème de marrons into a medium-sized bowl and whip them together until you get a pale and fluffy mixture that easily drops off the spoon (this is quicker with an electric hand whisk but can be done with a wooden spoon). Then add the eggs a little at a time, beating thoroughly after each addition.

Sift in the chestnut flour with the baking powder and use a large metal spoon to cut and fold the flour into the mixture, gradually adding the milk when about half is folded in. Divide the mixture as evenly as possible between the muffin cases and bake on the centre shelf of the oven for 35-40 minutes, or until they feel springy in the centre. Transfer to a wire rack. When the cakes have completely cooled, make up the topping by mixing the remaining crème de marrons with the mascarpone and spreading it equally over each cake. Then decorate with three slices of marron glacé on each and a light dusting of icing sugar.

These are best eaten as fresh as possible, and if you make them a day or so in advance it's best to put the topping on about half an hour before serving.

CHRISTMAS
PUDDINGS
and others...

I THINK IT IS sad to see old traditions die, and I'm sure there are many younger people who have never tasted a real home-made Christmas pudding. Factory versions sold in the shops are a million miles from a home-made version – a rich luscious combination of vine fruits, nuts and citrus peels laced with ale and rum slowly steamed into a dark fragrant mass of intense flavours. Still not convinced? No matter...there follows a very festive collection of puddings for every taste.

TRADITIONAL CHRISTMAS PUDDING
SERVES 10–12

This is quite definitely the best and, like the Christmas cake on page 29, has been made and loved by a cast of thousands over forty years. If you've never made a Christmas pudding, please don't be put off by the eight hours' steaming – it isn't any work, it just sits happily on its own getting the long slow cooking which is what gives it such wonderful flavour and character.

110g shredded suet

110g white breadcrumbs

1 level teaspoon ground mixed spice

¼ teaspoon nutmeg, freshly grated

a good pinch of ground cinnamon

225g soft dark brown sugar

110g sultanas

110g raisins

275g currants

25g whole candied peel, finely chopped

25g whole almonds, chopped (skin on is OK)

1 small cooking apple, cored and finely chopped (no need to peel)

the grated zest of ½ large navel orange

the grated zest of ½ large lemon

2 tablespoons rum

75ml barley wine

75ml stout

2 eggs

50g self-raising flour, sifted

A 1.2 litre pudding basin, lightly greased, baking parchment, foil and string, and a traditional or fan-type steamer.

Begin the day before you want to steam the pudding. Take your largest, roomiest mixing bowl and start by putting in the suet and breadcrumbs, spices and sugar. Mix these ingredients very thoroughly together, then gradually mix in all the dried fruit, peel and nuts followed by the apple and the grated orange and lemon zests. Don't forget to tick everything off as you go to make sure nothing gets left out. Next in a smaller basin, measure out the rum, barley wine and stout, then add the eggs and beat these thoroughly together. Next pour this over all the other ingredients and begin to mix very thoroughly. It's now traditional to gather all the family round, especially the children, and invite everyone to have a really good stir and make a wish! The mixture should have a fairly sloppy consistency – that is, it should fall instantly from the spoon when this is tapped on the side of the bowl. If you think it needs a bit more liquid add a spot more stout. Cover the bowl and leave overnight.

Next day stir in the sifted flour quite thoroughly, then pack the mixture into the lightly greased basin, cover it with a double layer of baking parchment and a sheet of foil and tie it securely with string (you really need to borrow someone's finger for this!). It's also a good idea to tie a piece of string across the top to make a handle. Place the pudding in a steamer set over a saucepan filled with simmering water and steam the pudding for 8 hours. Do make sure you keep a regular eye on the water underneath and top it up with boiling water straight from the kettle about halfway through the time. When the pudding is steamed, let it get quite cold, then remove the baking parchment and foil and replace them with some fresh ones, again making a string handle for easy manoeuvring. Now your Christmas pudding is ready for Christmas Day. Keep it in a cool place away from the light. Under the bed in an unheated bedroom is an ideal place. You'll find Christmas Day steaming instructions on page 266.

If you have any left over, it will reheat beautifully, wrapped in foil, in the oven next day. If you want two smaller puddings, use two 570ml basins, but give them the same steaming time. The best accompaniment is Christmas Rum Sauce (see page 266).

If you want to make individual Christmas puddings for gifts, this quantity makes eight 175ml pudding basins. Steam for 3 hours, then resteam for 1 hour before serving. They look pretty wrapped in baking parchment and muslin and tied with attractive bows and tags.

CHRISTMAS PUDDING (WITHOUT THE PUDDING) WITH MARSALA SYLLABUB

SERVES 6–8

This has all the traditional flavours of Christmas pudding packed into a Marsala wine and orange jelly. It is a delightfully cool dessert that slips down easily after a very rich main course. It also doubles up as a fruit compote on its own without the jelly, and can served either with the syllabub or spooned over vanilla ice cream.

FOR THE COMPOTE

75g no-soak dried apricots, cut into six

75g dried figs, cut into pieces the same size as the apricots

75g Agen no-soak prunes, cut into pieces the same size as the apricots

75g large Muscatel raisins

10g whole candied peel, finely chopped

¼ teaspoon mixed spice

¼ nutmeg, freshly grated

½ small Cox's apple, chopped (no need to peel)

the grated zest and juice of ½ small orange

the grated zest and juice of ½ small lemon

275ml Marsala wine

10g toasted flaked almonds

FOR THE JELLY

7g leaf gelatine (4 sheets measuring about 11 x 7.5cm each)

275ml smooth-style fresh orange juice

FOR THE MARSALA SYLLABUB

75ml Marsala wine

1 dessertspoon molasses sugar

150ml double cream

whole nutmeg

A 850ml pudding basin or six 175ml pudding basins or moulds.

Preheat the oven to 120°C/gas mark ½.

All you do to start off with is place all the compote ingredients (except the almonds) in a medium casserole. Place it over direct heat and bring to simmering point, then put a lid on and transfer it to the oven and leave to cook slowly for 3 hours. After that remove from the oven. Now, place the gelatine leaves in a bowl, cover with cold water and leave to soak for 5 minutes. After that squeeze the gelatine leaves and add to the hot compote, giving it a really good stir to distribute it evenly. Next add the nuts and orange juice, give it another good stir, and pour the mixture into the pudding basin then cool, cover and chill overnight, or until set.

For the syllabub, pour the Marsala into a bowl, add the sugar and leave aside for about 10 minutes to allow the sugar to dissolve. Then pour in the cream and whisk with an electric hand whisk until it stands in soft peaks. Cover and chill until needed.

To serve, remove the jelly from the fridge, dip the outside of the dish very briefly into hot water to loosen the jelly from the sides, and use a palette knife to release it all the way round. Place a large, flat plate on top and invert the dish and plate, allowing a minute or two before carefully removing the dish to leave the jelly turned out on the plate. Serve it at the table, cut into slices, with the syllabub, which looks nice with a little nutmeg grated over it.

CRANBERRY QUEEN OF PUDDINGS
SERVES 6-8

We often joke in our house about how, when the Christmas book was first published, the shops sold out of cranberries and for ages the press annoyingly referred to me as the Cranberry Queen. So, for old times' sake, we can relive the memory with this sublime English pudding made with those luscious berries I love so much.

850ml milk
20g butter
175g fresh white breadcrumbs
75g golden caster sugar, plus
    1 teaspoon extra
the grated zest of 1 large lemon
3 eggs
FOR THE CRANBERRY
COMPOTE
200g cranberries
40g golden caster sugar
the zest and juice of 1 small orange
½ teaspoon ground ginger
¼ teaspoon ground cloves
¼ teaspoon ground cinnamon

A 1.2 litre baking dish, generously
    buttered.

Preheat the oven to 180°C/gas mark 4.

First, pour the milk into a saucepan and bring to the boil then remove it from the heat and stir in the butter, breadcrumbs, 40g sugar and lemon zest. Leave it on one side for about 20 minutes to allow the breadcrumbs to swell.

Now separate the eggs, lightly beat the yolks and add them to the cooled breadcrumb mixture. Pour it all into the pie dish and spread it out evenly. Bake in the centre of the oven for 30-40 minutes, or until it's set in the centre.

While that's happening put all the cranberry compote ingredients into a medium saucepan, bring up to a gentle simmer and then, keeping the heat low, let it gently cook for about 25 minutes, or until nearly all the juice has evaporated. When the pudding comes out of the oven carefully spoon and spread the cranberry mixture all over.

Next, using an electric hand whisk, beat the egg whites in a large, scrupulously clean bowl until stiff, then whisk in the remainder of the caster sugar and spoon this meringue mixture over to the pudding. Finally, sprinkle the teaspoon of caster sugar all over it and bake for a further 18-20 minutes, or until the topping is golden brown.

STEAMED PANETTONE PUDDINGS WITH ELIZA ACTON'S HOT PUNCH SAUCE

SERVES 8

Panettone is an Italian fruit bread that's sold here mostly in the autumn and around Christmas time in beautifully designed boxes with carrying ribbons. If you would like a light but quite delectable alternative to Christmas pudding, this is it. I've tried making it in advance, freezing and then reheating it, and it works beautifully. But don't confine it to Christmas, as it's a truly great steamed pudding to serve at any time, especially with Victorian writer Eliza Acton's extremely alcoholic citrus sauce.

FOR THE STEAMED PANETTONE PUDDING

300g panettone
175g dried mixed fruit
3 tablespoons rum
50g whole candied peel, finely chopped
50g toasted flaked almonds
the grated zest of 1 orange
the grated zest of 2 lemons
50g molasses sugar
275ml milk
150ml double cream
3 eggs

FOR ELIZA ACTON'S HOT PUNCH SAUCE

1 large navel orange
1 lemon
110g caster sugar
25g plain flour
50g unsalted butter, softened
2 tablespoons rum
2 tablespoons brandy
175ml medium sherry

Either a double-pan steamer or a large saucepan with a fan steamer and a tight-fitting lid, eight 175ml pudding basins, well buttered, eight elastic bands, plus some foil or a 1.2 litre pudding basin, well buttered, some foil and string.

You need to begin this by soaking the dried mixed fruit in the rum overnight.

The next day, cut the panettone into 2.5cm chunks and place them in a large mixing bowl, along with the candied peel, flaked almonds, orange and lemon zests and the soaked, dried mixed fruit, plus any drops of rum that didn't get soaked up. Now give it all a really good stir to distribute everything evenly.

Then, in another bowl, whisk together the sugar, milk, cream and eggs and pour this all over the panettone, giving everything another good mix. Now pour the mixture into the buttered pudding basins and press everything down to pack it into each one. Cover the tops with a small double square of foil and secure them with an elastic band. Now boil a kettle and pour the boiling water into the saucepan, about half full, place it on a medium heat and, when it comes back to the boil, fit the steamer over the top.

Now stack the puddings into the steamer, put the lid on and steam the puddings for exactly 30 minutes (2 hours for a large pudding). Check the level of the water in the saucepan and, if necessary, top up with boiling water from time to time.

Meanwhile, make the hot punch sauce. First, prepare the orange and lemon zests, and to do this it's best to use a potato peeler and pare off the outer zest, leaving the white pith behind. What you need is four strips of each zest measuring approximately 5 x 2.5cm. Then, using a sharp knife, cut the strips into very thin, needle-like shreds. Now pop these into a medium-sized saucepan with the sugar and 275ml water, bring everything up to a slow simmer and keep it simmering as gently as possible for 15 minutes.

While that is happening, squeeze the juice from the orange and the lemon and, in a separate bowl, mix the flour and butter together to form a paste. When the 15 minutes are up, add the orange and lemon juice to the saucepan, along with the rum, brandy and sherry, and bring it all back up to a gentle simmer. Now add the paste to the liquid in small, peanut-sized pieces, whisking as you add them, until they have dissolved and the sauce has thickened. Serve the sauce hot in a warmed serving jug. If you make the sauce in advance, reheat it gently without boiling.

To serve the puddings, remove them from the steamer using tongs, then take off the elastic bands and foil and let them stand for 5–10 minutes, then slide a palette knife all around each one to loosen them and turn them out on to warmed plates. Pour some of the hot punch sauce over the puddings and carry to the table, with the rest of the sauce to hand round separately.

EIGHTEENTH-CENTURY CREAMED APPLE FLAN
SERVES 6

This recipe is a nostalgic one for me as it's one of the first I tried after some research into eighteenth-century British cooking at the British Museum, and it prompted me to do a whole lot more.

FOR THE FILLING

600g Bramley apples, peeled, cored and sliced
50g ratafia biscuits (or amaretti)
50g butter
2 tablespoons golden caster sugar
the grated zest of 1 small lemon
2 tablespoons brandy or cider
whole nutmeg
5 egg yolks
65ml double cream

FOR THE PASTRY

40g softened butter, cut into smallish lumps
40g softened pure lard
150g plain flour, sifted, plus a little extra for rolling out
(or 225g ready-made shortcrust pastry)

TO SERVE

icing sugar, to dust

A 19cm loose-based, fluted tart tin, 4cm deep, lightly greased.

Preheat the oven to 180°C/gas mark 4.

Mix the pastry by rubbing the fats into the sifted flour until the mixture resembles breadcrumbs, then add 1–2 teaspoons of water to make a dough that leaves the bowl clean. Pop the pastry into a polythene bag and leave to rest in the fridge for 30 minutes or so, then roll it out on a lightly floured surface and use to line the tart tin. Prick the base all over with a fork and brush with one of the egg yolks. Bake for 20 minutes.

Meanwhile, put the sliced apples in a saucepan with 2 tablespoons of water, cover and cook until they are pulpy. Transfer them to a large mixing bowl and beat until you have a smooth purée.

Now crush the biscuits: the best way to do this is to lay them flat inside a polythene bag, then roll them with a rolling pin to crush them into crumbs.

Whisk the butter and the caster sugar into the apple purée, followed by the biscuit crumbs, lemon zest, brandy or cider and a good grating of nutmeg. Combine everything thoroughly and leave the mixture to cool.

Next, whisk the remaining egg yolks together with the cream – don't overdo it, you just want them to thicken slightly. Then, when the mixture has cooled, stir the egg yolks and cream into it. Pour the whole lot into the partly cooked flan case and bake for a further 30–35 minutes.

Allow to cool, then chill for a couple of hours in the fridge before serving, dusted with icing sugar and some chilled pouring cream.

PANETTONE BREAD & BUTTER PUDDING WITH MARSALA
SERVES 6

In a way I'm very glad that the delectable Italian raisin and fruit bread, called Panettone, only comes into the house at Christmas. I absolutely love it and keep taking sneaky slices. It makes a splendid festive version of bread and butter pudding, like this.

400g panettone, cut into round slices,
    1.5cm thick
60g raisins
150ml Marsala
50g butter
20g whole candied peel, finely chopped
175ml milk
175ml double cream
60g golden caster sugar
the zest of 1 small lemon
4 eggs, beaten
½ whole nutmeg

A 1.5 litre baking dish, well buttered.

Begin by putting the raisins in a small saucepan with 50ml of the Marsala and bring them up to simmering point, then remove them from the heat then leave to soak and cool for about 40 minutes. Meanwhile, preheat the oven to 180°C/gas mark 4.

Then butter the slices of panettone and cut each one into quarters measuring about 6cm (if you are using the small panettone, just halve them). Now arrange a single layer of slightly overlapping slices in the prepared dish, saving all the nicest-looking pieces for the top. Next drain the raisins and reserve the liquid. Sprinkle half the raisins over the panettone and all of the candied peel. Now arrange the remaining slices of panettone on top, overlapping them attractively so the crusts are prominent, then sprinkle with the remaining raisins.

Next, in a large glass jug (it will need to be more than 570ml), measure out the milk, double cream, the remaining 100ml Marsala and the Marsala juices from the raisins. Now use a mini-whisk to whisk in the caster sugar, lemon zest and beaten eggs. Then pour the whole lot over the panettone and grate the nutmeg over the top. Pop the dish on a baking tray and bake for 50 minutes until the top is crisp and golden and the pudding is puffy and set in the centre. Leave it out of the oven to settle for 10 minutes, then serve with some chilled pouring cream or Marsala Syllabub (see page 49).

CHRISTMAS CRACKER PUDDINGS WITH MASCARPONE RUM CREAM
SERVES 6

This recipe comes from Jeff Baker, the chef at J Baker's Bistro Moderne in York. It was he who introduced me to this wonderful Tunisian pastry called *feuilles de brick*. It feels like lacy cloth with a satiny sheen and when baked has a soft and light crunchiness that's much nicer than filo.

3 individual luxury Christmas puddings (approx. 113g each or leftover Christmas pudding)
the grated zest of 1 medium orange
the grated zest of 1 lemon
7 sheets feuilles de brick (brick pastry)
1 tablespoon icing sugar
FOR THE MASCARPONE RUM CREAM
250g mascarpone
3 tablespoons dark muscovado sugar
3 tablespoons dark rum

A baking tray, lightly greased.

Preheat the oven to 180°C/gas mark 4.

First of all mix the rum with the muscovado sugar in a small bowl and leave it stand so the sugar has time to dissolve (about 30 minutes). Meanwhile turn out the Christmas puddings into a bowl along with the grated zests and mix well with a fork.

Now divide it into six equal portions and roll each one on a clean flat surface into a sausage shape (about 12cm in length). Next carefully peel one of the sheets of pastry away from its backing paper and lay it on a clean, dry surface. Then turn the first 6cm of pastry nearest to you inwards to make a fold.

Place one of the rolled pudding pieces centrally along the folded edge and roll it tightly away from you so you have a long cigar shape. Repeat the process with the remaining pastry and filling then arrange them, evenly spaced, on the baking tray. Now take the remaining sheet of pastry and, using a pair of scissors, cut 12 ribbons of pastry (1cm wide) from the centre of the pastry (so the ribbons will be longer). Next, pinch the pastry around both ends of each pudding and gently tie with a pastry ribbon – without pulling too tightly or it will break.

When all the crackers are tied pop the tray on the centre shelf of the oven and bake for 18 minutes. Meanwhile make the rum cream by combining the rum-and-sugar mixture with the mascarpone using an electric hand-whisk.

When the crackers are baked, let them stand for 10 minutes before cutting each one in half diagonally with a serrated knife. Serve them, one half-cracker leaning against the other, dusted with some icing sugar and Mascarpone Rum Cream on the side. Well-chilled whipped or pouring cream also makes a good accompaniment.

PICKLES, CHUTNEYS *and* PRESERVES

SUCH A BRITISH THING – the harvest produce of autumn preserved and tucked away in a cupboard to emerge in the darkest days of winter, and particularly at Christmas, when cold cuts abound and unexpected suppers are being called forth. Bite into a crisp sausage roll together with an equally crunchy pickled shallot! Spoon a generous helping of mustard pickle or intensely fruity chutney alongside a plate of cold meats together with some crisp celery and good bread – wonderful! And absolutely no cooking called for on the night. (Note: to sterilise preserving jars, wash them in warm soapy water, rinse and dry, then pop them in a medium oven for 5 minutes. Also you will also need some waxed discs for sealing the chutney and vinegar-proof lids.) Home-made pickles and chutneys keep indefinitely without refrigeration.

SPICED PICKLED PEARS
MAKES A 1 LITRE JAR

Pears in a mild spicy pickle make a really good accompaniment to Christmas cold meats or, I've found, to strong blue cheeses. If you warm them through slightly, they can also accompany a roast duck or goose. Their lovely amber colour makes them look very appealing and a very good choice for a home-made Christmas gift. If you want to make more, simply double or treble the recipe, remembering that 1kg of pears fills a 1 litre jar.

1kg Conference pears (the hardest and smallest you can find)
350g soft light brown sugar
275ml white wine vinegar
275ml cider vinegar
1 cinnamon stick, broken into three pieces
½ lemon, cut into thin slices
½ teaspoon whole cloves
1 teaspoon juniper berries
1 dessertspoon mixed pepper berries

Start off by putting all the ingredients except the pears in a large saucepan, then place it on a low heat, allowing it to come slowly to the boil. Give everything a whisk round from time to time to dissolve the sugar crystals.

While that's happening peel the pears. They need to be pared very thinly (forgive the pun). This means using either a very sharp knife or, best of all, a really good potato peeler. Take off all the peel but leave the stalks and the base florets intact. As you peel each pear, plunge it into a bowl of cold water. Then after peeling them, check that the sugar has completely dissolved into the vinegar, drain the pears and add them to the saucepan. Bring everything up to a gentle simmer and let the pears cook for about 10 minutes, then turn them over and simmer for another 10–20 minutes or until they look slightly transparent and feel tender when tested with a small skewer.

Using a draining spoon, transfer the pears and slices of lemon to the sterilised preserving jar (see page 61). Now boil the syrup furiously for about 5 minutes, until it's reduced to approximately 425ml, and pour in enough to fill the jar right up to its neck and completely cover the pears. Then scoop out the spices and add them to the jar as well. Any leftover syrup can be discarded. Cover with a waxed disc and seal the jar, and when the contents are completely cold, wipe and label it and store it in a cool, dark place for about 1 month before using. The pears will keep well for 6 months.

PICKLED SHALLOTS IN SHERRY VINEGAR
MAKES A 1 LITRE JAR

I can't eat a crisp, freshly baked sausage roll without an equally crunchy pickled onion or shallot. This used to be my late-night snack after Midnight Mass on Christmas Eve, but now I'm older, the dawn Mass is more appealing, so this ritual has been transferred to Christmas night.

450g pink shallots, peeled
570ml water
50g salt
175ml sherry vinegar
425ml white wine vinegar
1 tablespoon coriander seeds
1 small bird's eye chilli

You need to begin this 2 days ahead by placing the shallots in a 1.2 litre bowl. Then mix the water and salt together, pour over the shallots and leave them covered with a cloth for 2 days.

When you're ready to start pickling, bring the vinegars, coriander seeds and chilli up to simmering point in a saucepan, then leave them to get quite cold. Meanwhile drain the shallots in a colander, pat them dry with kitchen paper, then pile them into a 1 litre sterilised preserving jar (see page 61). Pour the cold vinegar (plus the spices) into the jar, seal it tightly and leave in a cool, dark place for 1 month before eating.

CHRISTMAS CHUTNEY
MAKES FOUR 350ML JARS

This has proved to be hugely popular since the first book was published. It is so-named because it is made with dried fruits which I always associate with Christmas: prunes, dates and apricots. It's dark, spicy and delicious with cold cuts, pork pies or hot sausages – and a dollop with potted meats and pâtés is highly recommended too.

350g no-soak prunes
275g pitted dates
275g no-soak dried apricots
450g onions, peeled
570ml cider vinegar
50g salt
1 dessertspoon grated fresh root ginger or
    1 heaped teaspoon ground ginger
75g allspice berries
450g demerara sugar

A large saucepan and a small piece of muslin or gauze.

The dried fruits and onions need to be chopped very small, and this can be done in a food processor. When they're all dealt with, put the vinegar in a large saucepan with the salt and the ginger, then tie the allspice berries up in the muslin or gauze very securely so they can't escape and add these to the pan. Bring everything up to the boil, then stir in the chopped dried fruits and onions, together with the sugar.

Leave it all to simmer very gently without a lid for about 1½ hours, or until the chutney has thickened. Stir from time to time during the cooking period. When it's ready you will be able to draw a spoon across the surface of the chutney and make a trail that doesn't immediately fill up with surplus vinegar.

Spoon the chutney into warm sterilised jars (see page 61), seal well with waxed discs and tight lids, and label as soon as it's cold. Keep this chutney for 1 month to mature in a cool, dark place before eating (but it will keep for years!).

SPICED PICKLED PRUNES IN ARMAGNAC
MAKES FOUR 350ML JARS

I have to say this is one of the staples at our restaurant at the football club, where it is served with every kind of pâté and terrine (we like it specially with the Duck Liver Pâté on page 103).

900g Agen no-soak prunes
1 tablespoon Lapsang Souchong tea
300ml good-quality red wine vinegar
125g light muscovado sugar
6 cloves
2 blades of mace
6 allspice berries
5 cinnamon sticks
4 tablespoons Armagnac

A medium-sized saucepan.

You need to begin the the night before. Measure 1.2 litres of boiling water into a jug, then stir in the tea and allow it to steep for 3 minutes. Meanwhile put the prunes into a large non-metallic bowl. Now strain the tea and allow it to cool completely before pouring it over the prunes. Cover the bowl with a clean tea towel and leave them to soak overnight.

Next day, put the vinegar along with the sugar and spices into a medium-sized saucepan, bring everything slowly up to the boil and allow to simmer for 15 minutes. Meanwhile drain off the tea and pack the prunes into warm sterilised jars (see page 61), filling them as full as possible. Now strain the liquid from the pan into a jug and carefully pour it over the prunes, swivelling the jars to make sure they are completely covered.

Finally spoon a tablespoon of Armagnac into each jar, then cover straightaway with a waxed disc and tight lids. When the prunes are cold, label the jars and store them in a dark place for at least one month – the prunes will get better as they mature.

PEAR & CRANBERRY CHUTNEY
MAKES THREE 350ML JARS

This lovely chutney has a history: it is served with game terrine at Christmas at our much-loved local pub, The Swan, at Monks Eleigh. It is actually made by a lady in the village called Ros Cohen and she has generously agreed to share her recipe with us. This is great with any kind of pâté, terrine or potted meat (see *Soups and Starters*, page 99).

500g pears (350g ripe, the rest under-ripe)
500g cranberries
1 cinnamon stick
1 heaped teaspoon allspice berries
225g chopped onions
250g light soft brown sugar
150ml distilled malt vinegar
the zest and juice of 1 orange

A large saucepan and a small piece of muslin or gauze.

First place the cinnamon and allspice in the muslin, tie it up with string and attach it to the handle of the pan. Next peel the pears, halve them and cut out the cores, then chop them into 1.5cm pieces. Now pile them in a large saucepan with all the other ingredients, give everything a good stir, then bring the whole lot up to the boil.

After that turn the heat down to simmer the chutney gently, stirring from time to time, for about 50–60 minutes, or until it has reduced to a thick pulp. Once a wooden spoon drawn across the surface of the chutney makes a channel that does not immediately fill up with vinegar, the chutney is ready. Now lift out the muslin bag and squeeze between 2 saucers to extract the juice, then stir the chutney well. Spoon the chutney into warm sterilised jars (see page 61), sealing well with waxed discs and tight lids while it's still hot. Label when cold and store in a cool, dark place for 1 month before eating.

ENGLISH MUSTARD PICKLE (PICCALILLI)

MAKES THREE 350ML JARS

This is as English as pork pie and very difficult to buy commercially – I've never found a good bought version except in small delis and farm shops. It's so good at Christmas with sausage rolls and cold cuts (and we love it with Brussels Bubble-and-Squeak! See page 190).

250g cauliflower, divided into
    2.5cm florets
175g small onions, quartered and cut
    across
200g cucumber, peeled, quartered
    lengthways and cut into 5mm slices
175g dwarf beans, cut into 2.5cm
    lengths
475ml malt vinegar, plus 2 tablespoons
    extra
¼ whole nutmeg, freshly grated
¼ teaspoon powdered allspice
75g caster sugar
1 clove garlic, crushed with ½ teaspoon
    salt
20g English mustard powder
10g turmeric
1 rounded tablespoon plain flour

First place the cauliflower florets, onions and 475ml vinegar together in a large saucepan, add the nutmeg and allspice and bring to the boil. Cover and simmer for 8 minutes. Now take the lid off and stir in the cucumber, beans, sugar and garlic. Bring the mixture up to simmering point again and cook for a further 5 minutes uncovered. The vegetables should still all be slightly crisp - so don't go away and forget them.

Now set a large colander over a large bowl and pour the contents of the saucepan into it and leave it all to drain (reserving the vinegar). Then mix the mustard powder, turmeric and flour together in a bowl. Gradually work in 2 additional tablespoons of vinegar and 1–2 tablespoons of water so that the mixture becomes a fairly loose paste. Next add a ladleful of the hot vinegar, drained from the vegetables, and transfer the blend to the saucepan. Bring to the boil, whisking with a balloon whisk, and gradually adding the remaining hot vinegar. Boil gently for 5 minutes, then transfer the vegetables from the colander to the large bowl, and pour over the sauce. Stir well to mix, then spoon the piccalilli into warm sterilised jars (see page 61) with waxed discs and tight lids. Keep for 2 months in a cool, dark place before eating.

SPICED CRANBERRY CHUTNEY
MAKES TWO 350ML JARS

This, as you would expect, is a lovely, bright, Christmassy colour, and it's excellent served with cold cuts, as well as sharp, assertive cheeses. Keep in a cool, dark place for a month before eating.

450g cranberries
2 cinnamon sticks
1 teaspoon ground cloves
2 tablespoons freshly grated root
  ginger
1 medium red onion, chopped
350g demerara sugar
the grated zest and juice of 2 oranges
425ml good-quality red wine vinegar
1 teaspoon salt

All you do here is place the ingredients in a wide, shallow pan. Bring everything up to simmering point and stir well, ignoring the scum that rises to the surface – it will soon disappear. Now, keeping the heat at a gentle simmer, let the chutney bubble and reduce for about 45 minutes, or until you can draw a wooden spoon across the surface and leave a trail that doesn't fill up with vinegar. Don't forget that it will thicken as it cools, so don't let it get too thick. Towards the end of the cooking time, sterilise the jars (see page 61), then fill them with the hot chutney (you can discard the cinnamon now). Cover with waxed discs, seal with lids and label when cold.

HOME-MADE CHRISTMAS MINCEMEAT
MAKES SIX 350ML JARS

Once again, over the years we have never found a match for this mincemeat recipe, so if I can persuade you to make it, you will never want the bought stuff ever again. It really is dead simple to make, though in the past people used to have trouble storing it. This was because the high percentage of apples oozed too much juice and the juice started to ferment. In the following recipe the mincemeat is placed in a barely warm oven and so the suet gradually melts and as this happens it coats all the fruits, including the apples, sealing in the juices. For a Traditional Mince Pie recipe, see page 78.

450g Bramley apples, cored and
    chopped small (no need to peel)
225g shredded suet
350g raisins
225g sultanas
225g currants
225g whole candied peel, finely
    chopped
350g soft dark brown sugar
the grated zest and juice of 2 oranges
the grated zest and juice of 2 lemons
50g whole almonds, cut into slivers
4 teaspoons mixed ground spice
½ teaspoon ground cinnamon
whole nutmeg, for grating
6 tablespoons brandy

All you do is combine all the ingredients, except for the brandy, in a large mixing bowl, stirring them and mixing them together very thoroughly indeed. Then cover the bowl with a clean tea towel and leave the mixture in a cool place overnight or for 12 hours, so the flavours have a chance to mingle and develop.

After that preheat the oven to 120°C/gas mark ¼, cover the bowl loosely with foil and place it in the oven for 3 hours. Then remove the bowl from the oven and don't worry about the appearance of the mincemeat which looks positively swimming in fat. This is how it should look. As it cools, stir it from time to time; the fat will coagulate and, instead of it being in tiny shreds, it will encase all the other ingredients.

When the mincemeat is quite cold stir in the brandy. Pack in sterilised jars (see page 61), cover with wax discs and seal. It will keep in a cool, dark cupboard indefinitely, but I think it is best eaten within a year of making.
NOTE Vegetarians can make this mincemeat happily, using vegetarian suet. And if you don't want the full quantity, make half.

DRINKS, MULLS *and* PARTY STUFF

CHRISTMAS MEANS PARTIES, and parties mean people. My own philosophy, which has not changed over the years, is that people are always more important than the food. So don't be afraid and remember everyone will enjoy being together first and foremost. The food should be good, of course, but simple and uncomplicated with as little last-minute preparation as possible. Drinks are also a big part of the celebration, so there needs to be something interesting for the drivers. You'll find it all here.

MULLED WINE
SERVES 10

Christmas carols, hot mulled wine and warm mince pies – the quintessential elements of a traditional English Christmas.

2 x 75cl bottles of a medium to full-bodied red wine
1 orange, studded with cloves
2 cinnamon sticks
4 oranges, sliced
8 tablespoons granulated sugar
whole nutmeg, for grating
2 tablespoons brandy

Put all the ingredients in a saucepan along with 1.2 litres of water, then bring up to simmering point, stirring until all the sugar has dissolved. Keep it at barely simmering point for at least 20 minutes – but do not boil or all the alcohol will evaporate. This can be made in advance, then reheated just before serving in mugs or sturdy wine glasses.

MULLED 'WINE' FOR DRINKERS
SERVES 10

Not the real deal, of course, but it looks the same and has a great flavour – and leaves you intact to drive home.

1 orange
½ lemon
a small orange, studded with cloves
175ml Belvoir Spiced Winter Berries Cordial
300ml freshly squeezed orange juice
1½ tablespoons honey
4 tablespoons golden caster sugar
1 cinnamon stick
2 star anise
½ teaspoon ground ginger

Begin by cutting the orange and lemon into slices. Now place all the ingredients in a large saucepan and add 1 litre of cold water. Stir together and simmer for 15–20 minutes to allow the flavours to infuse. Taste before serving and add more honey or sugar if needed. Ladle into mugs or heatproof glasses.

CRANBERRY COOLER
SERVES 6

For a cool, non-alcoholic party drink, this is the nicest we've found.

500ml chilled cranberry juice
500ml chilled red grape juice
500ml chilled ginger ale
1 large lime, cut into 6 wedges

All you need to do is pour the juices and ginger ale into a jug and give them a gentle stir. Pour into glasses containing lots of ice, squeeze half the juice from each lime wedge into each glass and drop the lime wedge into the glass as you do.

THE OXFORD BISHOP
SERVES 6-8

This wonderful mulled port recipe came originally from Eliza Acton, the great 19th-century cookery writer and the source of much of my inspiration. She says it can be made either with oranges or lemons, and having tried both, we think it's best with oranges.

1 whole orange
16 whole cloves
1 tablespoon sugar
½ teaspoon ground cinnamon
½ teaspoon ground mace
½ teaspoon allspice
¼ teaspoon ground ginger
75cl bottle of port
the juice of ½ orange
whole nutmeg

A small baking tray.

Preheat the oven to 200°C/gas mark 6.

Begin by cutting the orange in half and studding each half with 8 cloves, then place the halves on a baking tray in the centre of the oven to bake for 20 minutes.

Meanwhile, pour 275ml of water into a small saucepan, add the sugar, cinnamon, mace, allspice and ginger, then over a high heat bring the mixture to simmering point, giving it a good stir. Let it boil briskly until it has reduced by at least half, then take off the heat and leave on one side.

When you're ready to serve, empty the port into a saucepan and add the baked orange (plus the cloves). Pour in the spice mixture, followed by the orange juice, then heat gently without actually bringing to the boil. Serve it in a warmed bowl with the orange halves floating in it and a little grated nutmeg on top.

HOT SPICED CIDER WITH BUTTERED APPLES

MAKES 16 GLASSES

A glass of something warm and spicy goes very well with warmed mince pies during the party season.

2.25 litres still dry cider
4 small Cox's apples, cored (no need to peel)
25g butter, melted
1 tablespoon caster sugar
225g soft brown sugar
24 whole cloves
8 cinnamon sticks
16 allspice berries
the juice of 2 oranges
½ whole nutmeg, freshly grated

A medium baking sheet, lightly greased.

Preheat the oven to 190°C/gas mark 5.

First slice the apples into rings (you should get about 16 altogether), then brush each ring with butter and dust with a sprinkling of caster sugar. Place them on a greased baking sheet and bake on a high shelf in the oven for about 20 minutes – they should be softened but not floppy.

   Towards the end of that time, put all the other ingredients into a large saucepan and heat the mixture, stirring quite often, without letting it come to the boil. Finally add the apple rings. To keep it really hot without boiling, it's probably best to use a heat diffuser under the pan, then when you're ready to serve, ladle into warmed sturdy glasses (or glass tankards with handles) and place a slice of apple in each one. If you want to make it in advance, it's OK to reheat it gently – but again without letting it come to the boil.

TRADITIONAL MINCE PIES
with Cumberland Rum or Brandy Butter
MAKES 24

I will always cherish fond memories of my mother's and my grandmother's cooling trays piled high with freshly baked mince pies on Christmas Eve, ready to be packed into tins and brought out whenever friends popped in for Christmas drinks. The following is the traditional family recipe.

560g mincemeat (see page 70)
350g plain flour
a pinch of salt
75g lard
75g butter
FOR THE TOP
a little milk
icing sugar

One (or two) trays of 6cm patty tins,
    one fluted 7.5cm pastry cutter
    and one 6cm cutter.

Preheat the oven to 200°C/gas mark 6.

Make up the pastry by sifting the flour and salt into a mixing bowl and rubbing the fats into it until the mixture resembles fine crumbs. Then add just enough cold water to mix to a dough that leaves the bowl clean. Leave the pastry to rest in a polythene bag in the fridge for 20–30 minutes, then roll half of it out as thinly as possible and cut it into two dozen 7.5cm rounds, gathering up the scraps and re-rolling. Then do the same with the other half of the pastry, this time using the 6cm cutter.

Now grease the patty tins lightly and line them with the larger rounds. Fill these with mincemeat to the level of the edges of the pastry. Dampen the edges of the smaller rounds of pastry with water and press them lightly into position to form lids, sealing the edges. Brush each one with milk and make three snips in the tops with a pair of scissors. Bake near the top of the oven for 25–30 minutes until light golden brown. Cool on a wire rack and sprinkle with icing sugar. When cool, store in an airtight container.

CUMBERLAND RUM OR BRANDY BUTTER SERVES 8
Cumberland Rum Butter is excellent served with hot mince pies or Mincemeat & Apple Crumble Flan with Almonds (page 287). Brandy Butter is an alternative to serve with the Traditional Christmas Pudding (page 46).

175g unsalted butter, at room temperature
175g soft dark brown sugar
6 tablespoons rum or brandy

You can either blend the butter and sugar together till pale, soft and creamy in a food processor or else use an electric hand whisk. When you have a pale smooth mixture you can gradually add the rum or brandy a little at a time, beating well after each addition. Taste and add more rum or brandy if you think it needs it! Then place the butter in a container and chill thoroughly before serving. It is important, I think, to serve this very cold, so that it can provide a wonderful contrast to the hot mince pies or pudding. It will keep for 2–3 weeks in the fridge, so it's not really worth freezing.

PARMA HAM, PECORINO & ROSEMARY CRISPS
SERVES 4-6

This next recipe would be perfect for serving something home-made with pre-dinner drinks, and you can ring the changes with the type of cheese you use.

1 sheet feuille de brick (brick pastry –
 see page 59)
1 x 90g pack sliced Parma ham
75g grated Pecorino
1 tablespoon fresh chopped rosemary
freshly milled black pepper

A large baking tray, lightly greased.

Preheat the oven to 180°C/gas mark 4.

Begin by laying the sheet of pastry on a clean chopping board, then cover it loosely with Parma ham, leaving about 1cm of the lacy edge all round. Sprinkle the pecorino and rosemary as evenly as possible over the ham, and finish off with some freshly milled black pepper. Now take a very sharp knife and cut into 12 evenly sized wedges and arrange these on the baking tray.

Bake on the centre shelf for 12–15 minutes or until they are crisp and golden. Transfer them to a wire rack to cool and become very crisp.

PISTACHIO SABLES
MAKES ABOUT 30

This and the following recipe were kindly given to me by the Head Pastry Chef, Mark Mitson, at The Blakeney Hotel in Norfolk, where they are served in the bar with drinks, but only if you get there early enough, because they disappear in a flash.

15g shelled, unsalted pistachio nuts
40g strong white flour, sifted
40g unsalted butter, diced
40g freshly grated Parmesan
a pinch of cayenne pepper
seasoning

A large baking sheet, lightly greased.

Start by chopping the pistachio nuts in a mini chopper quite small. Then mix them with all the remaining ingredients in a medium-sized bowl. Rub the ingredients together until the mixture starts to form fairly large clumps, then press the mixture against the side of the bowl to bring it together.

Now transfer the dough to a board and knead lightly, then roll into a sausage shape about 18cm long and wrap and chill in the freezer for 30 minutes.

Preheat the oven to 180°C/gas mark 4. After that slice the chilled log into discs about 5mm wide and spread them out on the baking sheet.

Then pop them in the oven on the centre shelf and bake for 13-15 minutes, until they start to go golden around the edges. When they are cooked, transfer them to a wire rack to cool and store in an airtight tin.

GRUYÈRE & PARMESAN ALLUMETTES
MAKES ABOUT 80

This one, also courtesy of Mark Mitson, is another absolute winner to serve with drinks at Christmas or any time. I've never been keen on fiddly canapés, and these are so simple and easy, and absolutely never fail to please.

110g Gruyère, finely grated
25g freshly grated Parmesan
110g strong white flour, sifted
75g unsalted butter, diced
a pinch of cayenne pepper
seasoning
a little flour for rolling
a little beaten egg

Two baking sheets, lightly greased.

Preheat the oven to 180°C/gas mark 4.

First put the flour, Gruyère, butter and seasonings into a medium-sized bowl, then rub the ingredients together until the mixture starts to form fairly large clumps, then press the mixture against the side of the bowl to bring it together.

Transfer the dough to a flour-dusted board and knead lightly, then roll it to an oblong 21 x 31cm. Trim the edges to neaten them, then cut the dough into 2 pieces measuring 10 x 30cm. Brush the 2 oblongs of dough with beaten egg then sprinkle evenly with the Parmesan.

Now cut the dough into 'allumettes' 5mm x 10cm. Then use a pallete knife to lift them on to the greased baking sheets and spread them out a little. (You can knead the trimmings back together to make a few more allumettes.)

Bake them on the centre and lower shelves of the oven for about 15 minutes, swapping the baking sheets over about halfway through. When they are cooked, transfer to a wire rack and store in an airtight tin.

ETTY'S SAUSAGE ROLLS
MAKES ABOUT 24

Etty is my mum and for me a Christmas without her sausage rolls would not be complete. They are the ultimate canapé to serve with drinks, or with pickled shallots and crisp celery for a snack any time. They can be cooked well in advance, frozen then defrosted and warmed through when you need them, but nothing can compare with freshly baked on Christmas Eve.

FOR THE QUICK FLAKY PASTRY
175g butter or block margarine
225g plain flour
a pinch of salt
cold water to mix
(alternatively you can use 400g of
    ready-made all-butter puff pastry,
    which is almost as good)
FOR THE FILLING
450g good-quality pork sausagemeat
1 medium onion, grated
4 tablespoons chopped sage leaves
1 egg, beaten, to glaze

2 baking sheets, lightly greased.

Preheat the oven to 220°C/gas mark 7.

The fat needs to be rock-hard from the fridge, so weigh out the required amount, wrap it in a piece of foil and place it in the freezing compartment for 30–45 minutes. Meanwhile sift the flour and salt into a mixing bowl. When you take the fat out of the freezer, open it up and use some of the foil to hold the end with. Then dip the fat in the flour and grate it on a coarse grater placed in the bowl over the flour. Keep dipping the fat down into the flour to make it easier to grate.

At the end you will be left with a pile of grated fat in the middle of the flour, so take a palette knife and start to distribute it into the flour (don't use your hands), trying to coat all the pieces of fat with flour until the mixture is crumbly. Next add enough water to form a dough that leaves the bowl clean, using your hands to bring it all gently together. Put the dough into a polythene bag and chill it for 30 minutes in the fridge.

When you're ready to make the sausage rolls, mix the sausagemeat, onion and sage together in a mixing bowl. Then roll out the pastry on a floured surface to form an oblong approximately 42 x 30cm. Cut this oblong into three strips 42 x 10cm and divide the sausagemeat also into three, making three long rolls the same length as the strips of pastry (if it's sticky sprinkle on some flour and flour your hands).

Place one roll of sausagemeat on to one strip of pastry. Brush the beaten egg along one edge, then fold the pastry over and seal it as carefully as possible. Lift the whole thing up and turn it so the sealed edge is underneath. Press lightly, and cut into individual rolls each about 5cm long. Snip three V shapes in the top of each roll with the end of some scissors and brush with beaten egg. Repeat all this with the other portions of meat and pastry.

Place the rolls on baking sheets and bake high in the oven for 20–25 minutes, then remove them to a wire rack to cool. You can store the cooked and cooled sausage rolls in an airtight tin, but they do lose their crunchiness. For this reason I think it is preferable to freeze them in polythene boxes and remove a few at a time as and when you need them. Defrost them for an hour at room temperature and then warm them in a hot oven for 5 minutes.

CAVIAR CANAPÉS
MAKES 16

Not the real thing in this recipe (but it could be if you're very rich and want to splash out). These recipes alongside each other will be enough for 10-12 people.

1 x 135g pack of 16 cocktail blinis
3 eggs
1 rounded tablespoon soured cream or crème fraîche
1 rounded tablespoon fresh snipped chives
1 medium-sized shallot, peeled and very finely chopped
1 tablespoon butter, melted
1 x 50g jar lumpfish caviar (or Arënkha)
seasoning

Begin with the eggs by placing them in cold water, bringing them up to a fast boil, then timing them for 7 minutes. Then cool them under a cold running tap and peel off the shells. Now mash the eggs in a bowl with a fork, season and combine them with the cream, chives and freshly chopped shallot.

Next preheat the grill to high for 10 minutes. Melt the butter and brush the blinis lightly with the butter on both sides, then arrange them on a baking tray. When the grill's hot, place them about 10cm from the heat and time them for about 1½ minutes before flipping them over and giving them another 1½ to get them a little more golden and slightly toasted.

Let the blinis cool, then divide the egg mixture equally between them (starting with a heaped teaspoonful and topping up any that are a bit short). Finally spoon an equal quantity of caviar on top of each one.
NOTE These can be prepared a few hours in advance, covering them and keeping in the fridge. But you will need to remove them an hour before serving so they come back to room temperature.

BLINIS WITH SMOKED SALMON & SALMON CAVIAR
MAKES 16

These go very well side by side with the previous recipe, as the flavours are complementary to each other.

1 x 135g pack of 16 cocktail blinis
140g sliced smoked salmon
2 rounded tablespoons crème fraîche
1 tablespoon butter, melted
1 x 50g jar salmon caviar
a pinch of cayenne pepper
a few sprigs fresh dill

Prepare the blinis as in the previous recipe and, while they're cooling, divide the smoked salmon into sixteen pieces. Then divide them between the blinis folding them to fit neatly. Place a spoonful of crème fraîche on top of the smoked salmon, then spoon the caviar on top of that, dividing it as evenly as you can. Finish off with a dusting of cayenne on each one, along with a sprig of dill. If you are making these in advance, cover and chill as for the caviar canapés and put the dill on just before serving.

SPICED BROWN RICE SALAD WITH NUTS & SEEDS

SERVES 8-10

This is very colourful, with nuts and seeds giving lots of crunchy texture. The added plus is that it can be made well in advance and no last-minute attention. Just what you want for a party!

275ml brown basmati rice
    (as measured in a glass jug)
570ml boiling water
25g pecan nuts, roughly chopped
1 dessertspoon olive oil
3 spring onions, chopped small
    (including the green parts)
5cm cucumber, chopped small
    (no need to peel)
2 large tomatoes, skinned and chopped
    small
1 small green pepper, deseeded and
    chopped small
1 red apple, cored and chopped small
    (no need to peel)
40g currants
15g pumpkin seeds
25g shelled pistachio nuts

FOR THE DRESSING

1 small clove garlic
1 teaspoon salt
1 teaspoon mustard powder
1 dessertspoon Madras curry powder
2 dessertspoons white wine vinegar
freshly milled black pepper
4 tablespoons extra virgin olive oil

First of all heat the oil in a medium saucepan, then stir in the rice and toss it around to get the grains nicely coated with oil. Add some salt, then pour the boiling water over and bring it up to a gentle simmer. Stir once, then put the lid on and simmer gently for about 40 minutes or until the grains are tender.

Meanwhile, make the dressing by first crushing the garlic with the salt with a pestle and mortar, then add the mustard and curry powder, vinegar and some black pepper. Work these together using a mini-whisk, then add the olive oil and whisk very thoroughly.

Next preheat the grill for 10 minutes. Spread the pecan nuts out on a baking tray and toast them under the grill for about 2–3 minutes (without going away, as they burn very quickly!).

When the rice has cooked transfer it to a large salad bowl and, while it is still warm, mix in the dressing, making sure you do not break up the grains. Then leave it on one side to get quite cold before mixing in all the prepared vegetables, fruits and seeds. Taste to check the seasoning, then sprinkle the pecan and pistachio nuts on top. Cover and chill till needed.

WINTER POTATO SALAD
WITH MUSTARD DRESSING
SERVES 8-10

You could serve this warm or cold at room temperature. Either way it's great with cold cuts or as part of a buffet.

1kg small salad potatoes, or
   the equivalent of old potatoes
   cut into largish dice
salt
FOR THE DRESSING
2 tablespoons hot wholegrain
   mustard
2 tablespoons white wine vinegar
2 tablespoons extra virgin olive oil
TO SERVE
2 tablespoons chopped parsley or
   chives (or a mixture of both)
2 large spring onions (including the
   green parts), finely chopped
seasoning

Put the potatoes in a fan steamer in a saucepan, add boiling water from the kettle, sprinkle in a little salt and steam for 15-20 minutes. Meanwhile, whisk all the dressing ingredients together in a serving bowl. As soon as the potatoes are tender, transfer them to the bowl and toss them in the dressing while still warm, finally adding the herbs, spring onions and seasoning as required.

CHRISTMAS COLESLAW
SERVES 8–10

This is our favourite coleslaw, which we have improved from a recipe called 4-Star Slaw in the first book. If you mix the cabbage, celeriac and carrots with a little salt and lemon juice overnight it draws the excess liquid out of the vegetables, which means the finished salad keeps much longer, so you can make it well ahead.

225g celeriac, peeled and coarsely grated

225g carrots, peeled and grated

225g white cabbage, finely shredded

1 tablespoon lemon juice

salt flakes

6 spring onions (including the green parts), finely chopped

poppy seeds, to garnish

FOR THE DRESSING

150ml soured cream

2 cloves garlic, crushed

2 tablespoons mayonnaise

2 tablespoons natural yoghurt

1 teaspoon mustard powder

2 tablespoons olive oil

1 tablespoon white wine vinegar

1 tablespoon lemon juice

seasoning

The night before, place the prepared celeriac, carrots and cabbage in a large bowl with 1 tablespoon of lemon juice and 1 rounded teaspoon of salt. Toss them around, then cover the bowl and chill overnight. Next day drain the vegetables in a colander, place a clean tea towel over them and press well to get all the liquid out.

To make the dressing, combine the soured cream with the garlic, mayonnaise, yoghurt and mustard powder. Then mix together the oil, vinegar and lemon juice and gradually whisk these into the soured cream mixture. Taste and season as required. Then, to prepare the salad, simply put the vegetables in a bowl, pour over the dressing and toss with forks to mix thoroughly. Taste to see if it needs more seasoning, then cover and chill. Just before serving, toss the slaw again and sprinkle with the poppy seeds.

MINI TARTS WITH 3 TOPPINGS
TO MAKE 12 OF EACH

These are so easy and quick to make once you've assembled all the filling ingredients. They can be made ahead and warmed through in a hot oven for 3-4 minutes, or cooked and frozen, then reheated at 200°C/gas mark 6 for 6-7 minutes.

TOMATO, MUSTARD & THYME TARTS

100g butter puff pastry (ready-rolled if you like)

2 tablespoons Dijon mustard

4 cherry tomatoes, each trimmed of their ends and sliced into 3

1 sprig of thyme, torn into smaller sprigs

a little olive oil

a little flour

seasoning

A 4.5cm fluted cutter and a large baking tray, lightly greased.

Preheat the oven to 200°C/gas mark 6.

Begin by rolling out the pastry on a lightly floured surface to an oblong measuring about 23 x 18cm. Then cut out 12 x 4.5cm fluted rounds and arrange them slightly apart on the baking tray, then prick each one twice with a fork.

Now spread half a teaspoon of the mustard on each round and place a slice of tomato on top, then dip the thyme sprigs in olive oil and place one on each canapé. Finally season a little and bake on a high shelf for 18 minutes, until puffed and golden. Serve warm from the oven or just heated through.

GOAT'S CHEESE, RED ONION, OLIVE & THYME TARTS

This would work with any cheese. Mozzarella and Gruyère would both be good.

100g butter puff pastry (ready-rolled if you like)
40g hard goat's cheese, thinly sliced
¼ small red onion, chopped small
6 pitted black olives, halved
1 sprig of thyme, torn into smaller sprigs
a little olive oil
a little flour
seasoning

A 4.5cm fluted cutter and a baking tray, lightly greased.

Preheat the oven to 200°C/gas mark 6.

Begin by rolling out the pastry on a lightly floured surface to an oblong measuring about 23 x 18cm. Then cut out 12 x 4.5cm fluted rounds and arrange them slightly apart on the baking tray, then prick each one twice with a fork.

Cut the sliced goat's cheese into 2.5cm squares and place one of these on top of each pastry disc. Toss the onion in olive oil and sprinkle a little on top of each square of cheese, followed by half an olive. Then dip the thyme sprigs in olive oil and press these on top. Finally season a little and bake on a high shelf for 18 minutes, until puffed and golden. Serve warm from the oven or just heated through.

PARMESAN, SMOKED PANCETTA & SAGE TARTS

The smoky flavour of pancetta is best of all here, but thinly sliced smoked streaky bacon or Parma ham are also good.

100g butter puff pastry (ready-rolled if you like)

2 tablespoons freshly grated Parmesan

2 slices of smoked pancetta, each divided into 6 pieces

12 small sage leaves (or medium sage leaves cut in half diagonally)

a little olive oil

a little flour

seasoning

A 4.5cm fluted cutter and a baking tray, lightly greased.

Preheat the oven to 200°C/gas mark 6.

Begin by rolling out the pastry on a lightly floured surface to an oblong measuring about 23 x 18cm. Then cut out 12 x 4.5cm fluted rounds and arrange them slightly apart on the baking tray, then prick each one twice with a fork.

Now put ½ teaspoon of Parmesan onto each one then spread it out to the edge. Follow that with a piece of smoked pancetta, then dip the sage leaves in olive oil and they go on next. Finally, season a little and bake on a high shelf for 18 minutes, until puffed and golden. Serve warm from the oven or just heated through.

SOUPS *and* STARTERS

NOTHING HERE FOR CHRISTMAS DAY itself – in our book it simply isn't possible to eat a starter before such a rich and glorious feast. But as we've said, Christmas goes on for eight days and for other entertaining over the festive period we hope the following selection of first courses will hit the spot.

ARBROATH SMOKIE MOUSSE
SERVES 6

This is unashamedly retro. In the 60s it was very popular – only then made with smoked haddock (which is still equally good). It's cool, light and still evokes memories of that era.

1 pair of Arbroath smokies,
    about 400g (see page 15)
2 eggs
7g leaf gelatine (4 sheets measuring
    about 11 x 7.5cm each)
10g butter
200ml milk
10g sauce flour
125g mayonnaise
a good pinch of cayenne
3 tablespoons fine capers
2 tablespoons chopped parsley
50ml double cream, lightly whipped
seasoning
TO SERVE
30g watercress
2 tablespoons fine capers
cayenne pepper

Six ramekins with a base measurement
    of 7.5cm, lightly oiled.

Begin with the eggs by placing them in cold water, bringing them up to a fast boil, then timing them for 7 minutes. Then cool them under a cold running tap and peel off the shells. Now remove the skin and bones from the smokies (they will come away very easily), then flake the flesh into small pieces and chop the eggs similarly. Next soak the gelatine leaves in a bowl in cold water and in a medium saucepan, place the butter, milk and flour. Whisk these continuously together over a medium heat so the mixture will gradually thicken as it comes up to a simmer. Then leave it on the barest simmer for 3–4 minutes, stirring often.

After that remove it from the heat, squeeze the excess water from the gelatine then whisk the gelatine into the hot sauce to dissolve it – which will happen quite quickly. Now transfer the sauce to a bowl, let it cool for about 10 minutes before stirring in the mayonnaise and cayenne and seasoning well.

Next stir in the smokie pieces, eggs, capers and parsley, then finally fold in the whipped cream. Divide the mixture equally between the ramekins, cover them with clingfilm and chill for several hours. When you want to serve them, remove from the fridge 30 minutes before, then slide a small palette knife round the edge of each one and turn out onto serving plates. Give each one a dusting of cayenne and a sprinkling of capers on top and garnish with watercress.

DUCK LIVER PÂTÉ WITH ARMAGNAC
SERVES 6

I wish we could buy duck livers all the year round, but thankfully they are at least around at Christmas, and they make a wonderfully smooth, velvety pâté. At other times this recipe works just as well with chicken livers.

225g duck livers, rinsed and trimmed
225g butter
2 tablespoons Armagnac
2 teaspoons mustard powder
¼ teaspoon ground mace
1 teaspoon chopped fresh thyme
2 cloves garlic, crushed
seasoning
FOR THE GARNISH
6 small sprigs fresh thyme
6 juniper berries

Six ramekins with a base diameter of
    5.5cm (or six similar-sized
    pots).

To make the pâté, take a medium-sized, heavy-based frying pan, melt about 25g of the butter in it and fry the duck livers over a medium heat for about 5 minutes. Keep them on the move, turning them over quite frequently. Then remove them from the pan with a draining spoon and transfer them to a blender or food processor.

Now, in the same pan, gently melt 150g of the remaining butter and add this to the blender or food processor. Then pour the Armagnac onto the juices left in the frying pan (to capture all the lovely flavours) and pour that over the livers. Now add the mustard, mace, thyme, garlic and some seasoning. Leave to stand for 10 minutes, then blend until you have a smooth, velvety purée.

Next, divide this between the ramekins (or pots) and use some damp kitchen towel to clean the edges. Then melt the remaining 50g of the butter, pour a little over each one to seal, press in a sprig of thyme and a juniper berry, and leave them to get quite cold. Cover with clingfilm and place in the fridge till needed.

Don't forget to remove from the fridge about an hour before serving as the pâté needs to be eaten at room temperature. This is good served with Spiced Pickled Prunes in Armagnac (see page 65) or Marmalade of Apples, Raisin & Shallots (see page 107).

SCALLOPS IN THE SHELL
SERVES 6

Fresh scallops are very plump and good around Christmas time, and this is my own favourite way of serving them. The recipe has the advantage of requiring no last-minute fuss – it even freezes well and can be cooked straight from the freezer.

6–8 large, plump scallops,
    with their corals if possible
425ml dry vermouth
75g butter (plus 10g extra
    for the sauce)
1 small onion, finely chopped
175g button mushrooms, sliced
50g plain flour
225ml double cream
3 tablespoons white breadcrumbs
1½ tablespoons freshly grated
    Parmesan
seasoning

Six large scallop shells or 6 heatproof
    china scallop dishes (or similar),
    well buttered.

Start by slicing the white parts of each scallop into rounds about 5mm thick, and put the corals on one side. Now to poach the scallops: pour the Vermouth into a deep frying pan and bring it up to a gentle simmer, then pop the scallops in and, when it comes back to simmering point, cook for exactly 30 seconds. Remove them with a draining spoon to a plate and poach the corals for 1 minute and transfer them to join the scallops (reserving the poaching liquid to make the sauce).

Now melt 75g of butter in a medium saucepan and add the onion and let it cook over a medium heat for a few minutes, then add the mushrooms and some seasoning, turn the heat down and let them cook gently for about 15 minutes. After that sprinkle in the flour and stir to soak up all the juices, add the poaching liquid very gradually, stirring continuously till you have a thick smooth sauce, then continue to simmer gently for 4-5 minutes.

After that take the pan off the heat and stir in the extra 10g of butter and the double cream, taste to check the seasoning and leave on one side to cool. When it's cooled, stir in the poached scallops and the corals, and divide the mixture between the prepared dishes. Combine the breadcrumbs with the Parmesan and sprinkle all over, before covering with clingfilm and chilling till needed.

Before serving preheat the oven to 200°C/gas mark 6, then place the shells on a baking tray and cook on the centre shelf for 30 minutes from the fridge, or 45 minutes from frozen, until they are golden brown and starting to bubble at the edges.

POTTED PORK WITH JUNIPER & THYME
with a Marmalade of Apples, Raisins & Shallots
SERVES 8

It's good to bring some forgotten traditional English recipes – like potted meats and terrines – into Christmas. If they're tucked away in the fridge, there's always something special to hand for those 'other' mealtimes.

400g minced pork
50g smoked streaky bacon, chopped
    small
1 clove garlic, crushed
⅛ teaspoon ground mace
1 heaped teaspoon chopped thyme
    leaves
8 juniper berries
½ teaspoon whole black peppercorns
1½ tablespoons brandy
½ teaspoon salt
FOR THE GARNISH
some sprigs of thyme
a few juniper berries

A 570ml pudding basin.

Preheat the oven to 150°C/gas mark 2.

All you do here is place the meats, garlic, mace and thyme in a mixing bowl. Then, using a pestle and mortar, crush the juniper berries and peppercorns – not too finely. Add these, along with the brandy and salt, then give everything a really thorough mixing. Now pack the mixture into the bowl, press the thyme sprigs and juniper berries onto the surface, then cover with double sheet of foil, twisting it to make a kind of lid.

Place it on a baking tray then into the oven to cook slowly for 1½ hours. Then remove it from the oven, place some scale weights (or something else heavy) on top to firm it up and leave to get quite cold before transferring to the fridge. Serve cut into wedges, straight from the bowl.

MARMALADE OF APPLES, RAISINS & SHALLOTS SERVES 8
This also goes well with any other pâté, terrine or pork dish.

350g Cox's apples (no need to peel)
250g shallots, peeled and halved if large
50g raisins
⅛ teaspoon whole cloves
½ teaspoon ground cinnamon
⅛ nutmeg, freshly grated
275ml strong dry cider
55ml cider vinegar
25g dark muscovado sugar

To prepare the apples, core and cut them into quarters, then slice each quarter into three. Place them, along with all the other ingredients, in a medium-sized saucepan, bring everything up to a gentle simmer and just leave it to cook very gently (without a lid) for 50–60 minutes, until the liquid has reduced and the mixture looks sticky and glossy. If you want to make this in advance, to serve just warm it through gently – it doesn't need to be hot, just warm.

POTTED VENISON WITH PORT
with Spiced Cranberry & Orange Marmalade
SERVES 6

Cubed casserole venison is fine for this and the suppliers on page 15 will provide an excellent service if you have trouble finding it.

300g casserole venison
110g smoked streaky bacon
1 clove garlic, crushed
⅛ teaspoon ground mace
½ teaspoon cayenne pepper
⅛ teaspoon ground allspice
½ teaspoon salt
1½ tablespoons port

A 570ml pudding basin or
    heatproof bowl.

Preheat the oven to 170°C/gas mark 3.

The venison can be carefully pulse-chopped in a food processor or by hand if you prefer – but in any event it needs to be chopped small. Then it goes into a bowl with the rest of the ingredients and needs a very thorough stir. After that pack it into the pudding basin, cover it with a double sheet of foil (twisted at the edges), place it on a baking tray in the oven for 1½ hours.

After that, remove it from the oven, and weight it down with scale weights (or some other heavy object) on top to firm it up until it's cold. Then transfer to the fridge till needed. Serve cut into wedges straight from the bowl, with the Spiced Cranberry & Orange Marmalade.

SPICED CRANBERRY & ORANGE MARMALADE
SERVES 6

In France this would be a confit; in England it's a marmalade. Either way it is extremely good to serve with potted meats and terrines.

450g cranberries
the grated zest and juice of 1 orange
½ teaspoon ground cinnamon
¼ teaspoon ground cloves
1 level teaspoon ground ginger
75g golden caster sugar
175ml red wine
2 tablespoons red wine vinegar

All you do here is place the ingredients in a medium-sized saucepan, bring everything up to simmering point and simmer very gently for about 40 minutes without a lid, until the liquid has evaporated into a sticky syrup and almost disappeared.

PHEASANT TERRINE
SERVES 10-12

This is a kind of rough country pâté and it's perfect for a busy household at Christmas, because it means there's always something sublime sitting in the fridge for a snack supper or lunch. For smaller numbers it's a good idea to stick half in the freezer, where it will stay really good for up to a month.

340g pheasant thigh meat (or breast)
800g minced pork
225g pig's liver
275g smoked streaky bacon
15 juniper berries (and a few extra for the top)
½ teaspoon black peppercorns
1 rounded teaspoon salt
½ teaspoon ground mace
2 fat cloves garlic, crushed
1 heaped teaspoon thyme, chopped
150ml dry white wine
25ml brandy
bay leaves

A 1.75 litre terrine or 900g loaf tin.

Begin by cutting the pheasant, bacon and liver into rough pieces, then place them in the food processor bowl and process carefully (with the pulse button) until quite finely chopped – it looks messy and unattractive at this stage but no matter. Next tip the meats into a large mixing bowl and mix them together very thoroughly. Now coarsely crush first the juniper berries and then the black peppercorns in a pestle and mortar and add these to the meat, along with 1 heaped teaspoon of salt, the mace, garlic and thyme. Now you need to mix again even more thoroughly to distribute all the flavours evenly. After this, add the wine and brandy and give it a final mix, then cover the bowl with a cloth and leave it in a cool place for a couple of hours to allow the flavours to be absorbed.

Before cooking the terrine, preheat the oven to 150°C/gas mark 2. Then pack the mixture into the terrine or loaf tin and decorate the top with the bay leaves and the extra juniper berries. Place the terrine or tin in a roasting tin half-filled with hot water on the centre shelf of the oven and leave it there for about 1¾ hours. By the time it has cooked, the pâté will have shrunk quite a bit. Remove it from the oven and allow it to cool without draining off any of the surrounding juices; once the pâté has cooled, the fat and jelly will keep it beautifully moist.

Now cover the terrine with double foil and use some weights to press it down until it is quite cold – this pressing isn't essential but it helps to make the pâté less crumbly if you want to serve it in slices. If you don't have any scale weights, use any heavy object: bricks, tins of food or any innovation you can think of instead. If you don't weight it, you can serve it in chunks rather than slices. When it is cold, store in the fridge – it does get better with keeping for 24 hours before serving.

To serve the pâté you need to take it out of the fridge at least 30 minutes ahead, to return it to room temperature. Take slices out of the terrine and serve with cornichons, watercress and hot toasted or chargrilled bread, or some very crusty fresh bread. It's also good with Spiced Pickled Prunes in Armagnac (see page 65), Pear & Cranberry Chutney (see page 65) or Marmalade of Apples, Raisins & Shallots (see page 107).

WILD MUSHROOM & WALNUT SOUP
SERVES 8

Walnuts are at their best at Christmas time and, together with some dried wild mushrooms, can be used to make an unusual soup for a dinner party or a warming lunch or supper snack with some good cheese to follow.

25g dried porcini mushrooms
275ml boiling water
50g butter
110g dark-gilled mushrooms,
    roughly chopped
2 medium carrots, chopped
2 celery stalks, chopped
1 medium onion, chopped
1 leek, washed and chopped
2 bay leaves
1½ teaspoons chopped fresh thyme
2 cloves garlic, crushed
2 litres vegetable stock (made with
    Marigold bouillon)
TO FINISH
225g small open-cap mushrooms,
    keep 4 whole and chop the
    rest finely
25g butter
110g walnuts, ground in a nut mill or
    food processor
75ml single cream
75ml dry sherry
1 dessertspoon lemon juice
seasoning

First place the dried mushrooms in a jug with 275ml boiling water and leave them to soak for 30 minutes. Meanwhile, in a large saucepan, melt the 50g butter, then add all the prepared vegetables, herbs and garlic, stir well over a gentle heat until everything is glistening with a coating of butter, then pour in the dried mushrooms and their soaking water, followed by 2 litres of hot stock. Then bring up to a gentle simmer and, keeping the heat low, let the soup barely simmer for 1 hour.

After that, place a colander over a large bowl and strain the soup into it. Remove the bay leaves, and purée the vegetables with a little bit of the stock in a liquidiser or processor, then return this to the rest of the stock and whisk to a smooth consistency.

Now wipe out the soup saucepan with some kitchen paper and return it to the heat with the 25g butter. Lightly sauté the chopped mushrooms for about 5 minutes. After that, pour in the soup mixture, stir in the ground walnuts and some seasoning, and let it continue cooking gently for 10 minutes. While that's happening, use your sharpest knife to slice the 4 reserved whole mushrooms into wafer-thin slices for a garnish.

When you are ready to serve the soup, stir in the cream, sherry and lemon juice and serve piping hot with the slices of raw mushroom floating on top and if you like a few croutons, see the recipe on page 112.

FENLAND CELERY SOUP WITH STILTON
SERVES 6

So named after the famous Fenland 'dirty' celery, which is in quite a different league from most varieties. Its flavour is exquisite and, if you're lucky enough to find some, it is perfect for serving with cheese at Christmas. Soup-wise, any variety is better than none!

450g celery (1 large head, trimmed weight)

50g butter

1 potato (about 200g), peeled and diced

1 small onion, finely chopped

570ml vegetable stock (made with Marigold bouillon)

150ml single cream

150g Stilton

seasoning

FOR THE CROUTONS

110g thickly sliced stale white bread, crusts removed and cut into small cubes

2 tablespoons olive oil

First of all separate the stalks of celery from the base and trim, reserving the leaves for a garnish – the trimmed stalks should weigh 450g. Trim off the outer stringy bits, then scrub the rest in cold water, drain them, then slice across into thinnish slices.

Now, in a medium saucepan, melt the butter and stir in the celery, potato and the onion. Stir everything around to get a good coating of butter, then put a lid on the pan and, keeping the heat low, allow the vegetables to sweat for ten minutes to release their buttery juices. Then uncover and pour in the stock and bring it up to simmering point. Cover again and cook gently for 30 minutes; after that test that the vegetables are tender and, if not, re-cover and continue to cook until they are.

While that's happening you can prepare the croutons. Heat the oil in a large frying pan, then add the cubes of bread and toss them around (keeping them constantly on the move), until they have turned a deep golden-brown colour and become very crisp and crunchy. Drain on kitchen paper.

Next remove the saucepan from the heat and stir in the cream, then liquidise the soup along with the crumbled cheese until it is quite smooth. Return the soup to the rinsed-out pan and reheat very gently (because the soup, at this stage, should not be boiled). Taste and season if necessary, then serve the soup sprinkled with the chopped celery leaves and crisp croutons.

CHESTNUT SOUP WITH BACON & SAGE CROUTONS
SERVES 6

In the original Christmas book, a similar recipe to this one had the instructions on how to prepare and peel chestnuts. Not my favourite task! Now thankfully we can buy them ready prepared and frozen – brilliant!

400g frozen peeled chestnuts, defrosted (or vac-packed)
1½ sticks celery, chopped
1 medium onion, chopped
1 medium carrot, chopped
1 litre vegetable stock (made with Marigold bouillon)
seasoning

FOR THE CROUTONS
110g thickly sliced stale white bread, crusts removed and cut into small cubes
2 tablespoons olive oil
2 rashers of bacon, very finely chopped
1 tablespoon chopped sage leaves

To make the soup, you simply place all the ingredients in a large saucepan, season, bring up to simmering point, then put a lid on and simmer very gently for 25 minutes.

While that's happening you can prepare the croutons. Heat the oil in a large frying pan and cook the bacon gently for 5 minutes. Then turn the heat up to its highest setting, add the cubes of bread, together with the sage, and toss them around (keeping them constantly on the move) until they, and the bacon, have turned a deep golden-brown colour and become very crisp and crunchy.

Turn them out on to some absorbent kitchen paper. Then, as soon as the soup is ready, transfer it to a blender and purée until smooth. Reheat it in the rinsed-out pan and serve in warmed soup bowls, with the croutons, bacon and sage sprinkled over.

DUCK, GEESE *and* GAME

THE AIMS OF THIS chapter are twofold. First it is for people who don't want to go down the turkey route on Christmas Day, and secondly it is for those who do but might like something different on the other days – quite a few of these recipes for game can be made in advance and tucked away in the freezer till they are needed.

POT-ROASTED GUINEA FOWL WITH CALVADOS, CREAM & APPLES
SERVES 2–3

There are some lovely plump, free-range guinea fowl around at Christmas and this would be a splendid celebration lunch or supper for two or three. If you don't have Calvados, use brandy (but as Calvados is such a lovely ingredient to always have by in the kitchen, Christmas is a good excuse to buy a bottle!).

1 plump, free-range guinea fowl
1 tablespoon butter
2 tablespoons Calvados
2 shallots, peeled and finely chopped
1 clove garlic, chopped
3 medium-sized Cox's apples (no need to peel)
175ml dry cider
1 teaspoon chopped sage, plus a few extra sage leaves
150ml double cream or crème fraîche
seasoning

A large, deep saucepan with a tight-fitting lid and a ladle.

Begin by heating the butter in the saucepan over a medium heat until it foams, then season the bird and brown it in the hot butter, turning it frequently so it can brown all over (use a cloth to protect your hands as you turn it).

At this stage – when the bird is sitting upright again – warm the Calvados in a ladle over direct heat, then turn the flame out and set light to the warm Calvados using a long match and pour it over the guinea fowl. (If you do not have a gas hob, warm the Calvados in a small saucepan.) When the flames have died down, add the shallots and garlic and, keeping the heat low, let them soften while you prepare the apples. Remove the cores and cut them into 1cm rings. As you slice them, add them to the pan, tucking them all around.

Now pour in the cider, add the chopped sage and some seasoning, put a tight-fitting lid on and let it cook very gently for 1 hour. When the bird is cooked, remove it to a carving board and cover. Simmer the apples till the liquid has almost evaporated, then add the cream to the apples, giving it all a good shake, then turn the heat out. Carve the guinea fowl the same way as pheasant (see page 121) onto a serving platter and spoon the apples and a few sage leaves all over.

ROAST STUFFED GOOSE WITH APPLES & PRUNES IN ARMAGNAC

SERVES 8

Nineteen years in print and it's quite simply the best recipe for goose that I know. It has a classic English forcemeat stuffing made with the goose liver along with pork, sage and onion, with a second spicy prune and apple stuffing, and then it's finally served with prunes that have been soaked in Armagnac. All this together makes a wonderful combination of flavours. Serve it with crunchy roast potatoes and Traditional Braised Red Cabbage (see page 195).

1 young goose with giblets, weighing
  4.5–5.5kg oven-ready
a little wine for the gravy
salt and freshly milled black pepper
FOR THE PRUNES IN
ARMAGNAC
350g no-soak prunes
150ml Armagnac
50g granulated sugar
FOR THE APPLE STUFFING
700g Bramley apples, cut roughly into
  1cm slices
225g no-soak prunes, roughly chopped
1 large onion, roughly chopped
2 tablespoons Armagnac
⅛ teaspoon ground cloves
¼ teaspoon ground mace
seasoning
FOR THE FORCEMEAT
STUFFING
the goose liver, finely chopped
1 Cox's apple, cored and finely chopped
  (no need to peel)
275g minced pork or good-quality pork
  sausagemeat
1 medium onion, finely chopped
50g breadcrumbs
1 tablespoon chopped sage
seasoning

A large roasting tin with a rack and a
  small skewer.

Preheat the oven to 220°C/gas mark 7.

You can prepare the prunes several days in advance. Pop them in a saucepan with the Armagnac and sugar. Bring up to simmering point, then cool, cover and keep in the fridge.

Make the apple stuffing by mixing all the ingredients together and make the forcemeat stuffing, too, by mixing all the ingredients together.

When you are ready to cook the goose, begin by placing the forcemeat stuffing into the neck flap end of the bird, pressing it in as far as you can, tucking the neck flap all round it and patting it with your hands to make a rounded shape. Secure the flap underneath with a small skewer. Next, place the apple stuffing in the body cavity as it is – although it looks raw and chunky, after cooking it will collapse to a fluffy mass.

Season the goose well with salt and pepper, lay it on a rack in a roasting tin, then place it in the centre of the preheated oven. Give it 30 minutes' initial cooking, then reduce the temperature to 180°C/gas mark 4 and roast another 3 hours. That is for a 5kg goose plus stuffing; allow 15 minutes less for a 4.5kg bird, 15 minutes more for a 5.5kg one. Meanwhile, make a stock with the giblets (see page 255).

When the goose is cooked the juices will run clear if you pierce the thickest part of the leg with a skewer. Remove the bird to a serving dish, snap off the wing tips and allow to rest for 20 minutes or so before serving.

Now drain off the fat from the tin and make a rich dark gravy from the remaining residue, the giblet stock and a little wine. Then heat the prunes gently in a frying-pan and transfer them to a warmed serving dish. After carving the goose give each person a little of each of the stuffings, and serve the gravy and prunes separately.

TRADITIONAL ROAST PHEASANTS WITH MADEIRA GRAVY & BREAD SAUCE
SERVES 4

Roasting pheasants in butter muslin is the best way I've come across if you want to guarantee them to be moist and tender. Do remember, though, to check with your supplier that the pheasants are young enough to roast. Older birds should always be braised or casseroled. Just one pheasant cooked in this way would make a wonderful Christmas lunch for two people (or if you cooked two the other bird would be excellent served cold on other days).

1 brace of pheasants weighing about 700g each
4 rashers of unsmoked streaky bacon
110g butter, at room temperature
a few sprigs of fresh thyme
2 bay leaves, snipped into 4 pieces
seasoning
FOR THE GRAVY
a little plain flour
stock made with the pheasant giblets (see page 255)
1 teaspoon redcurrant jelly
2 tablespoons Madeira
seasoning
TO SERVE
1 half-quantity Traditional Bread Sauce (see page 266)

Two pieces of muslin 45 x 45cm, some wooden cocktail sticks and a medium-sized roasting tin.

Preheat the oven to 230°C/gas mark 8.

Wipe the birds with some kitchen paper and trim off any odd bits of skin that are hanging loose. Then, beginning at the neck cavity of each bird, pinch the skin to loosen it and provide a kind of pocket along each side of the breast. Next insert the pieces of bacon, snipping them in half if you need to, so that what you end up with is breast covered by bacon covered by skin.

Place each pheasant in the centre of a piece of muslin, season and plaster each pheasant with butter spread thickly all over. Wrap the muslin up like a parcel, bringing two opposite edges up, one over the other, then tuck the thyme and bay leaves in and finally fold the other two edges over and secure the parcels at both ends with cocktail sticks.

Now place the birds in a roasting tin on a high shelf in the oven and give them 30 minutes, then reduce the heat to 190°C/gas mark 5 and continue to cook the pheasants for a further hour, basting with the butter from time to time. When a pheasant thigh is pierced with a skewer and the juices run clear it's done. Discard the muslin and leave the birds to rest in a warm place whilst you make a gravy.

Spoon off all the excess fat from the roasting tin and place the tin over a medium heat. Stir in a little flour till smooth, then gradually add enough stock to make a thinnish sauce. Season and let the gravy bubble and reduce before stirring in the redcurrant jelly and Madeira. Carve the pheasants (see page 121) and serve with the gravy and bread sauce.

POT-ROASTED PHEASANTS IN MADEIRA
SERVES 4

In the original recipe a brace of pheasants were cut up into portions, but that is quite a bit of work. So we've found it easier this time to cook the pheasants whole and carve them before serving.

1 brace of pheasants weighing about
    700g each
25g butter
1 tablespoon groundnut oil
200g dry-cured lardons
450g shallots, peeled
1 medium whole carrot, trimmed and
    peeled
1 stick of celery (with leaves), cut into 3
250g small open-cap mushrooms
    (or portabellini)
2 large cloves garlic, peeled
425ml dry white wine
570ml Madeira
3 sprigs thyme
2 bay leaves
1 tablespoon plain flour mixed with
    1 tablespoon soft butter
seasoning

A 4.5 litre heavy-based casserole.

Season the pheasants all over, then melt the butter and oil in the casserole and when it starts to sizzle, add the pheasants and brown them all over, turning them around in the hot fat with a cloth to protect your hands. This will take about 15 minutes. After that remove them to a dish and leave on one side.

Now, keeping the heat high, brown the lardons, and remove them. Follow with the shallots and, after they've browned, return the pheasants and lardons to the casserole and add the carrot, celery, mushrooms, garlic, wine, Madeira, thyme, bay leaves and some seasoning then bring it all up to simmering point, turn the heat down to the very gentlest simmer, put the lid on and cook for 1¼ hours.

After that transfer the pheasants to a warmed dish and, using a draining spoon, remove the rest of the ingredients to join them, discarding the carrot, celery, garlic, bay leaves and thyme. Then add the butter-and-flour mixture in ½ teaspoon-sized lumps to the sauce, and whisk until it comes back to simmering point and thickens slightly. Now return the shallots, lardons and mushrooms to the hot sauce while you prepare the pheasant.

To carve the pheasant put one of the birds on its back on a board, take a sharp knife and run the blade down the breastbone and along the wishbone, keeping it as close to the bone as you can. Using the knife as a lever, gently pull the breast away from the frame. Now insert your fingers along the ribcage and you'll find you can ease the leg and thigh away from the bone. Trim the bits of skin off and repeat with the other side. Do the same with the second pheasant, and finally cut each half in half again and return to the casserole to warm the joints in the sauce before serving. Purée of Potato & Celeriac with Garlic (see page 186) would be a good accompaniment.

VENISON SAUSAGES BRAISED IN WHITE WINE WITH CARAMELISED CHESTNUTS
SERVES 4-6

You could make this with any kind of good quality sausages, but venison seems more festive. Needless to say, a pile of fluffy mashed potato or Purée of Potato & Celeriac with Garlic (see page 186) goes down a treat with this.

700g venison sausages

1 tablespoon groundnut or flavourless oil

450g smoked bacon lardons

450g small shallots, peeled

1 teaspoon coriander seeds

1 teaspoon salt flakes

1 teaspoon black peppercorns

2 cloves garlic, chopped

550ml dry white wine

1 dessertspoon chopped thyme

2 bay leaves

300g frozen peeled chestnuts, defrosted (or vac-packed)

25g butter

½ teaspoon golden caster sugar

400g small open-cap mushrooms (or portabellini)

20g plain flour mixed with 20g soft butter

A large flameproof casserole and a large heavy frying pan.

First heat the oil in the casserole, then, with the heat turned down to medium, brown the sausages evenly all over, taking care not to split the skins by turning them over too soon. Then, using a draining spoon, transfer them to a plate while you brown the bacon along with the shallots. This will take about 8-10 minutes. Now crush the coriander, salt and peppercorns together with a pestle and mortar (not too finely, so they are still fairly coarse), then add them to the casserole along with the garlic.

When the bacon and shallots have become golden brown, return the sausages to the casserole and add the white wine, thyme and bay leaves. Now bring everything up to a gentle simmer, put a lid on the casserole, turn the heat down as low as possible and let it simmer for 45 minutes.

Meanwhile, caramelise the chestnuts - to do this, heat the 25g butter in the frying pan until it bubbles, then stir in the chestnuts and fry for 5-6 minutes, until they are crisp and deep golden brown in colour. Then stir in the sugar and cook for a further 2 minutes before removing the pan from the heat and keeping on one side.

After the initial 45 minutes add the mushrooms to the casserole and push them down into the sauce and simmer for a further 15 minutes without the lid so that the liquid can reduce slightly.

When the time is up, using a draining spoon, transfer the sausages and all the vegetables etc. to a warm serving dish. Then whisk the butter and flour mixture into the sauce and let it bubble for a few minutes till thickened. Then reserve 30 of the chestnuts (for serving) and add the rest to the sauce, and use either a stick blender or a liquidiser to whiz them till smooth. Then return everything to the pan and bring back to simmering point.

Reheat the reserved chestnuts, then serve the sausages on warmed plates sprinkled with the chestnuts.

MUSTARD RABBIT BRAISED IN CIDER
SERVES 4

Farmed rabbit was never a good idea, but thankfully wild rabbit is now much more widely available and comes conveniently jointed ready for cooking. We have also tried this with chicken, which is equally good.

4 rabbit joints weighing about 600g
1 tablespoon made-up mustard
4 rashers of smoked streaky bacon
225g onions, roughly sliced
2 medium leeks, washed and sliced
175g Chantenay carrots, leave whole
1 dessertspoon thyme leaves, plus a
    few sprigs of thyme
1 dessertspoon chopped parsley
1 clove garlic, chopped
1 bay leaf
275ml strong dry cider
1 tablespoon cider vinegar
seasoning
TO FINISH
2 egg yolks
1 teaspoon cornflour
150ml double cream or crème fraîche
1 dessertspoon grain mustard

A large flameproof casserole with a
    tight-fitting lid.

Preheat the oven to 140°C/gas mark 1.

First spread the made-up mustard over the rabbit joints, then season them and wrap a piece of bacon round each one. Now in a flameproof casserole arrange half the onions, leeks, carrots and chopped herbs, then place the rabbit joints on top. Sprinkle in the garlic, then arrange the rest of the vegetables and sprigs of thyme on top along with some seasoning. Add the bay leaf, pour in the cider and cider vinegar, cover with a tight-fitting lid and place the casserole in the oven for 3 hours.

After that use a draining spoon to remove the rabbit joints and keep them warm. Whisk the egg yolks and cornflour together in a bowl till smooth, add the cream and grain mustard and whisk again. Now place the casserole over direct heat and bring the juices up to a gentle simmer while you whisk in the cream mixture until the sauce has thickened. Serve the rabbit and vegetables with the sauce poured over. Creamy mashed potatoes would be a good accompaniment.

VENISON BRAISED IN GUINNESS & PORT WITH PICKLED WALNUTS
SERVES 6–8

This is dark, rich and luscious and needs lots of fluffy mashed potato to absorb all the exquisite sauce. It's perfect, too, for entertaining as it braises slowly in the oven so you can forget about it until your guests arrive. All you need to do is remember to start the marinade the night before. It's also equally good made with beef.

1.5kg venison or beef, cut into
    2.5cm squares
700ml Guinness (or other stout)
150ml ruby port
1 x 400g jar pickled walnuts, drained
    and halved
1 bay leaf
2 sprigs of fresh thyme
1½ tablespoons butter
1½ tablespoons olive oil
1 large onion, chopped
1 large clove garlic, crushed
1 rounded tablespoon plain flour
seasoning

A large flameproof casserole with a
    tight-fitting lid.

The night before, you need to place the meat in a large bowl along with the bay leaf and thyme, then pour the Guinness and port all over it. Put a plate on top to keep the meat pushed down and leave in a cool place overnight.

Next day, when you are ready to cook the meat, preheat the oven to 140°C/gas mark 1. Then melt half the butter and oil in the casserole and heat gently. Drain the meat (reserving the liquid and herbs) and dry a few pieces at a time with kitchen paper. Now turn the heat to high and add a few pieces of venison to the casserole to brown them (if you add too much in one go they will release too much steam and not brown sufficiently). As soon as they are browned, remove them and continue until all the meat is browned. Now add the rest of the butter and oil to the casserole. As soon as it begins to foam, add the onion and brown this for about 8 minutes before adding the garlic and frying for another 2 minutes.

Now return all the meat into the casserole to join the onions. Stir in the flour to soak up the juices, then pour in the marinade (including the bay leaf and thyme), add the walnuts and season well. As soon as it reaches a gentle simmer, put a lid on, then transfer the casserole to the middle shelf of the oven and forget all about it for 3 hours, by which time the meat will be tender and the sauce marvellously dark and rich.

ROAST DUCK WITH CHERRY SAUCE
SERVES 4

After 40 years of recipe writing about other more elegant ways of serving duck I have now returned to this, the original recipe. If you think halfway to Chinese this is what it's like, moist flesh, lots of lovely very crispy bits and I still can't believe it's so simple.

1 oven-ready duck weighing 2.25–2.7kg
salt flakes
freshly milled black pepper
watercress, to garnish
FOR THE SAUCE
275g top-quality morello cherry jam
    (Tiptree is good)
225ml red wine

A roasting tin with a roasting rack or
    some foil.

Preheat the oven to 220°C/gas mark 7.

Prepare the duck by wiping it as dry as possible with kitchen paper. Then, using a small skewer, prick the fatty bits of the skin, particularly between the legs and the breast. Now either place it on the roasting rack in the tin or make a rack yourself by crumpling the foil and placing it in the bottom of the roasting tin. Season with salt flakes and freshly milled black pepper, using quite a lot of salt, as this encourages crunchiness.

Now place the tin on a highish shelf of the preheated oven.

After 20 minutes turn the heat down to 180°C/gas mark 4, then basically all you have to do is leave it alone for 2½ hours (or 30 minutes longer for a 2.7kg bird). During the cooking time, using an oven glove to protect your hands, remove the tin from the oven and drain the fat from the corner of the tin – do this about 3 times (the fat is brilliant for roast potatoes, so don't throw it away).

To make the sauce, simply combine the jam and wine and bring it up to a simmer then simmer for about 10 minutes to thicken slightly.

When the cooking time is up the duck skin should sound crisp when it is tapped with a knife, if it's not pop it back in the oven for a bit longer. then when it's cooked, allow it to rest for 5 minutes or so, then divide it into portions. All you need to do is cut the bird in half lengthways (i.e. along the length of the breast and either side of the backbone) with a sharp knife, then cut the halves into quarters (you may need some help with kitchen scissors here), leaving any escaped pieces of bone behind.

Serve with the sauce poured around so as not to lose the crispness of the skin and garnish with watercress.

Other
MAIN COURSES

I MAY BE A turkey traditionalist, but I can highly recommend ribs of Aberdeen Angus beef for a splendid, very special Christmas lunch for those who want a change from poultry. Equally, the other recipes in this chapter have been selected for alternative entertaining any time during the Christmas season.

ROAST COLLAR OF BACON WITH BLACKENED CRACKLING *with Cumberland Sauce*
SERVES 4 (WITH LEFTOVERS FOR THE CHRISTMAS HOLIDAY)

This is what I always traditionally cook on Christmas Eve because not only is it exquisite served hot with all its crunchy crackling and my favourite English sauce, it also sees us through the rest of the holiday served cold alongside turkey and other cold cuts. However, in one go, on its own, it will serve 12 people.

2.25kg collar of bacon (or gammon if
    you prefer)
1 tablespoon molasses or black treacle
salt flakes

A solid, medium-sized shallow
    roasting tin.

Preheat the oven to 240°C/gas mark 9.

First of all, using a very sharp pointed knife, score the skin of the bacon in a criss-cross pattern, making little 1cm diamonds (insert the tip of the knife only, hold the skin taut with one hand and drag the tip of the knife down in long movements).

To cook the bacon: warm the molasses or black treacle slightly (if it's very cold) then use a pastry brush to lightly coat all the little diamonds. Next, sprinkle the skin with salt flakes, pressing them well in, then place the joint in a roasting tin skin-side up (if it won't stand straight, use a couple of wodges of foil to prop it up).

Place the roasting tin in the oven and after 25 minutes turn the heat down to 180°C/gas mark 4, and continue to cook for a further 1¾–2 hours. It should feel tender all the way through when tested with a skewer. Leave it to rest for at least 30 minutes after coming out of the oven.

Serve with Traditional Braised Red Cabbage (see page 195) and Cumberland Sauce (see page 132), which is always served at room temperature.

NOTE If you have a larger or smaller piece of bacon (or gammon) calculate 25 minutes per 450g total cooking time.

CUMBERLAND SAUCE SERVES 8

1 medium lemon
1 medium orange
4 heaped tablespoons good-quality redcurrant jelly
   (Tiptree is best)
4 tablespoons port
1 heaped teaspoon mustard powder
1 heaped teaspoon ground ginger

First, thinly pare off the zest of both the lemon and the orange using a potato peeler, then cut into very small strips 1cm long and as thin as possible. Boil them in water for 5 minutes to extract any bitterness and drain well.

Now place the redcurrant jelly in a saucepan with the port and melt, whisking them together with a mini whisk over a low heat for 5 or 10 minutes.

In a serving bowl, mix the mustard and ginger with the juice of half the lemon until smooth, then add the juice of the whole orange, the port and redcurrant mixture, and finally the zests. Whisk well and the sauce is ready to use. Cumberland Sauce keeps well in a screw-top jar in the fridge for up to 2 weeks.

SLOW BRAISED BELLY PORK WITH BACON, APPLES & CIDER
SERVES 6

This is a very special recipe which could make a great meal for the family on Christmas Eve. Once assembled, it sits happily in a slow oven for three hours, leaving you free to attend to other things.

900g belly of pork (6 thick cut slices)
250g smoked dry-cured streaky bacon
    (12 slices)
3 medium Cox's apples (no need
    to peel)
1 large or 2 medium onions
3 fat cloves garlic
18 juniper berries
18 sage leaves
225ml dry cider
55ml cider vinegar
1 dessertspoon lard (or oil)
seasoning

A large flameproof casserole with a
    tight-fitting lid.

Preheat the oven to 140°C/gas mark 1.

In a large flameproof casserole heat the lard to smoking hot. While it's heating trim off any excess fat from the outer edges of the pork and season them on both sides. Now brown them well on both sides, three at a time, and remove them to a plate before doing the same with the slices of bacon (no seasoning this time).

While that's happening, slice the onions into thick rings, then they can follow the bacon (adding a little more fat or oil if needed). They too should be well browned on both sides. Meanwhile, peel and slice the garlic, crush the juniper berries with a pestle and mortar, and core the apples with an apple corer, and slice each one into four thick rings.

When the onions are ready, remove them to a plate then, off the heat, wipe the casserole with kitchen paper. Now arrange the onion over the base, followed by the pork. Sprinkle in the garlic and juniper, and follow this by laying the bacon slices on top of the pork. Next scatter the sage leaves here and there, then arrange the apple slices on top.

Now pour in the cider and cider vinegar and add a little seasoning. Then fit a lid, using a sheet of foil as well to make it really tight. Place the casserole in the centre of the oven for 3 hours. Traditional Braised Red Cabbage (see page 195) and mashed potatoes would be the perfect accompaniments.

ROAST RIBS OF ABERDEEN ANGUS BEEF
with a Confit of Whole Garlic & Shallots
SERVES 6–8

For those underwhelmed by turkey, Christmas is a time to splash out on a really good, well-hung joint of the best Aberdeen Angus. The confit is superb to serve with it and is something really different from the usual horseradish.

a three-rib piece of trimmed sirloin of beef (about 2.7kg)
1 small onion, peeled and halved
1 dessertspoon mustard powder
1 dessertspoon plain flour
425ml red wine
freshly milled black pepper

FOR THE GRAVY
1 heaped tablespoon plain flour
570ml vegetable stock (from potatoes or other vegetables)
300ml full-bodied red wine

A medium roasting tin.

Preheat the oven to 240°C/gas mark 9.

Place the beef, just as it is, upright in a roasting tin, tucking in the onion halves alongside it. Combine the mustard powder and flour, then dust this all over the surface of the fat, and finally season with a few twists of freshly milled pepper. This floury surface will help to make the fat very crusty (for those like me who want to eat what I call the 'crispies'), while the onion will caramelise to give the gravy a rich colour and flavour. Place the joint in the oven – it will have plenty of fat, so don't add extra.

After 20 minutes turn the heat down to 190°C/gas mark 5 and continue to cook for 15 minutes per 450g for rare, plus 15 minutes extra for medium rare or 30 minutes extra for well done. While cooking, baste the meat with the juices at least three times. To see if the beef is cooked to your liking, insert a thin skewer and press out some juices: the red, pink or clear colour will indicate to what stage the beef has cooked.

Remove the cooked beef to a board for carving and leave it to rest for at least 30 minutes before serving (while it's resting you can increase the heat in the oven to finish the roast potatoes if you're serving them). This resting period allows most of the juices which have bubbled up to the surface of the meat to seep back in and the meat itself firms up to make it easier to carve.

To make the gravy, spoon off most of the fat from the corner of the tilted meat tin. Place over a medium heat and sprinkle the flour into the fatty juices. Then, with a wire whisk, blend in the flour using a circular movement. When you have a smooth paste, slowly add the vegetable stock, whisking all the time and scraping the base of the tin to incorporate all the residue from the roast. Once the gravy has started to bubble, add the red wine. Let the gravy continue to bubble and reduce very gently, then taste to check the seasoning. Turn the heat down low and, after you have carved the beef, add any escaped juices to it before pouring into a warmed serving jug.

CONFIT OF WHOLE GARLIC & SHALLOTS

600g small, even-sized shallots, peeled and left whole
375ml dry red wine
50ml red wine vinegar
18 large cloves garlic, peeled
1 dessertspoon golden caster sugar
seasoning

A lidded, shallow pan with a base measurement of about 24cm.

Place the shallots, wine and vinegar in the pan and bring everything up to a simmering point. Then cover with the lid and let it simmer very gently for 25 minutes. After that time, turn the shallots over in the pan and add the garlic, poking it down into the liquid between the shallots, then continue to simmer, uncovered this time, for 30 minutes. After this time check the shallots are tender with a skewer and if they are not give them a little longer, then sprinkle in the sugar and increase the heat a little for a final 10 minutes, so the juices have reduced to a glaze that coats the shallots. Taste and season if necessary. If it's more convenient, the confit can be made ahead and reheated gently before serving.

FILLET OF BEEF IN PASTRY WITH WILD MUSHROOMS & RED WINE SAUCE
SERVES 6

This is an update of an old personal favourite of mine. It's easy to prepare and is equally good served cold on a buffet table – I've even taken it on a picnic! Its other virtue is that it can be prepared well in advance and just popped in the oven when you're ready. I've also included a horseradish sauce recipe, if you want to serve it cold.

800g middle cut or thick end fillet
    steak in one piece
300g ready-made all-butter puff pastry
15g dried porcini mushrooms
1 large onion
325g dark-gilled open-cap mushrooms
40g butter
whole nutmeg
1 teaspoon of beef dripping or
    groundnut oil
a little brandy
a little flour, for rolling
1 egg, beaten
seasoning
FOR THE RED WINE SAUCE
275ml full-bodied red wine

A heavy baking sheet, lightly greased.

Begin by making the filling well ahead – it needs to be chilled before you use it. Soak the porcini in boiling water for 20 minutes and while that's happening chop up the onion and open-cap mushrooms as finely as possible (if you have a food processor you can do this in moments; if not use a very sharp knife and chop them minutely small). When the porcini have had their 20 minutes, squeeze out all the excess liquid (and reserve it for later), then chop them small as well. Now, in a medium saucepan, melt the butter and stir in the onions and mushrooms to get a good buttery coating, then season and add a few gratings of fresh nutmeg.

What you need to do now is turn the heat to its lowest setting and cook, uncovered, allowing the juices to evaporate slowly. This will take about 35 minutes altogether – stir from time to time and what you should end up with is a lovely concentrated mixture with no liquid left. Spoon the mixture into a bowl, cool and chill in the fridge.

Now season the beef well, then heat the dripping in a frying pan over a high heat. When it is smoking hot, add the beef and brown it on all sides (using a cloth to protect your hands as you turn it). The browning will take about 5 minutes or so, then remove it to a plate and brush it all over with brandy, then leave it on one side to cool.

Now, with the frying pan still on the heat, add the reserved mushroom soaking liquid and let it bubble and reduce a bit, then add the red wine, a heaped tablespoon of the mushroom mixture and some seasoning. Reduce the heat and let it all simmer and reduce by about a third, then take it off the heat and reserve till you need it.

When both the mushrooms and beef have cooled, roll the pastry on a lightly floured surface to a rectangle approximately 35 x 25cm. Trim the edges (keep the trimmings for decoration), then spread one-third of the mushroom mixture over the centre, just large enough for the beef to sit on, then place the fillet on top and cover with the remaining mushroom mixture and pat it down round the beef into a good shape.

Now brush the edges of the pastry with beaten egg and wrap the pastry like a parcel around the meat. If necessary brush the edges at each end with a little more egg before folding them in. Now turn it over so the seal is underneath and use any trimmings to make pastry leaves for decoration. Now place it on a plate and cover and chill in the fridge till needed.

When you're ready to cook the beef, preheat the oven to 230°C/ gas mark 8. Place the beef parcel on a greased baking sheet and brush the pastry all over with beaten egg. Bake in the oven for 35 minutes for medium-rare beef, or 5 minutes less for rare and 5 minutes more for well done. When it comes out of the oven, warm the sauce while you rest the beef for 10 minutes before serving it cut into 6 thick slices. Alternatively cool it completely, chill and serve cold as part of a buffet with Horseradish, Crème Fraîche & Mustard Sauce.

HORSERADISH, CRÈME FRAÎCHE & MUSTARD SAUCE

4 rounded tablespoons hot horseradish sauce
2 heaped tablespoons crème fraîche
2 dessertspoons grain mustard

Simply mix the ingredients together and put them into a serving bowl.

ROAST LOIN OF PORK WITH CRACKLING & A CONFIT OF SPICED PRUNES & APRICOTS
SERVES 8

This recipe originated from a brilliant chef called Matt Kemp at The Underground Cookery School at St Mary's Church, London EC2. His loin was boned and rolled, then cut into beautiful slices, but this version is, I think, easier for home cooks.

2.25kg loin of pork, chined (but with the chine bone attached)
1 small onion, peeled
1 tablespoon plain flour
275ml dry cider
275ml vegetable stock (made with Marigold bouillon)
salt flakes and freshly milled black pepper

FOR THE CONFIT
225g Agen no-soak prunes
225g no-soak dried apricots
8 shallots, peeled and each one cut though the root
450ml strong dry cider
100ml cider vinegar
1 heaped tablespoon soft dark brown sugar
¼ teaspoon ground cloves
¼ teaspoon ground mace
2 cinnamon sticks, broken into pieces

A medium solid roasting tin.

Preheat the oven to 240°C/gas mark 9.

While the oven is preheating, score the skin of the pork (it will be scored already, but it's always best to add a few more lines). To do this, you can use the point of a very sharp paring knife and what you need to do is score the skin all over into thin strips, bringing the blade of the knife about halfway through the fat beneath the skin.

Now place the pork in a tin, skin-side up, halve the onion and wedge the two pieces in slightly underneath the meat. Next take about 1 tablespoon of crushed salt flakes and sprinkle it evenly over the skin, pressing it in as much as you can. Then place the pork on a high shelf in the oven and roast the joint for 25 minutes. After that turn the heat down to 190°C/gas mark 5 and calculate the cooking time, allowing a total of 35 minutes per 450g. In this case it would be a further 2½ hours and there's no need to baste pork as there's enough fat to keep the meat moist.

While the pork is cooking you can make up the confit, which is oh, so simple. All you do is place all the ingredients in a medium saucepan, bring everything up to a gentle simmer, while giving it a good stir. Then let it simmer gently (stirring once or twice) for about an hour, until most of the liquid has evaporated into a sticky mass. It can be made in advance and gently reheated if you need to (cold leftover pork with cold confit is also very good!).

The way to tell if the meat is cooked is to insert a skewer into the thickest part and the juices that run out should absolutely clear, without any trace of pinkness. When the pork is cooked, remove it from the oven and give it at least 30 minutes' resting time before carving. While that is happening, tilt the tin and spoon all the fat off, leaving only the juices. The onion will probably be black and charred, which gives the gravy a lovely deep colour. Leave the onion in, then place the roasting tin over direct heat, turned to low, sprinkle in the flour and quickly work it into the juices with a wooden spoon.

Now turn the heat up to medium and gradually add the cider and the stock, this time using a balloon whisk, until it comes up to simmering point and you have a smooth, rich gravy. Taste and season, then discard the onion and pour the gravy into a warmed serving jug. Serve the pork carved into slices, giving everyone some crackling with the confit.

Celebration
SEAFOOD

THE FIRST CHRISTMAS BOOK did not contain a section on seafood but now times have changed, with, I suspect, more people not wanting meat (at least some of the time). So I hope the recipes that follow will prove you *can* still celebrate with seafood!

SEAFOOD LASAGNE
SERVES 4-6

If you're going to have a busy time at Christmas, it's so useful to have all these ingredients tucked away in the store cupboard and freezer. If you need them – fine. If you don't, they'll all be there for another day.

250g frozen raw tiger prawns
200g frozen shelled cooked mussels
200g frozen scallops
175g frozen baby squid
1 tablespoon extra virgin olive oil
2 shallots, peeled and chopped
1 large clove garlic, peeled and crushed
1 small red chilli, deseeded and finely
    chopped
165ml dry white wine
175g ripe tomatoes, peeled, deseeded
    and chopped
200g fresh lasagne sheets (which can
    be frozen)
seasoning
FOR THE BÉCHAMEL
845ml milk
50g butter
50g plain flour
1 bay leaf
whole nutmeg, for grating
¼ teaspoon ground mace
seasoning
TO SERVE
1½ tablespoons extra virgin olive oil
squid tentacles (see recipe)
1 clove garlic, peeled and crushed
1 tablespoon chopped parsley

A baking dish with a base
    measurement 18cm x 23cm,
    5cm deep, well buttered.

First of all, spread the frozen shellfish out on a large plate with a double sheet of kitchen paper and leave to defrost for 1–1½ hours. Then slice the scallops fairly thickly into rounds (about 5mm thick). Now heat 1 tablespoon of olive oil in a medium-sized pan and cook the shallots with the garlic and chilli gently for about 5 minutes.

Meanwhile, pull the squid tentacles away from the body and keep them reserved in the fridge until later. Then cut the squid into 1cm rings. After that add the wine to the shallots, turn the heat up and let it bubble and reduce for about 10 minutes, until it has almost completely evaporated, then add the tomatoes and cook for 5 minutes more, until the tomato softens to a pulp. Season well before stirring in all the shellfish (except the tentacles) and remove from the heat.

Now make the béchamel by placing the milk, butter, flour, bay leaf, about a quarter of the nutmeg grated, mace and seasoning in a medium-sized saucepan over a medium heat then, whisking all the time, slowly bring it up to simmering point until the sauce has thickened. Then turn the heat down to its lowest setting and let it simmer for about 5 minutes.

Preheat the oven to 180°C/gas mark 4. Now you can assemble the lasagne, so spread a large spoonful of the béchamel over the base of the dish, then cover with some sheets of lasagne, cutting them with scissors to fit the dish evenly (rather than overlapping them). Spread a third of the fish mixture over the pasta, followed by about a quarter of the remaining béchamel, then continue to layer everything, finishing off with a layer of pasta covered with the remaining béchamel sauce.

Bake the lasagne in the oven for 40–45 minutes, until the sauce is bubbling and the top is golden brown. When you remove it from the oven, leave it to rest for 10 minutes and, while that's happening, heat 1½ tablespoons of olive oil in a small frying pan, then add the squid tentacles and garlic and sauté gently for 2 minutes. Stir in the parsley and some seasoning, then sprinkle this mixture (and all the juices from the pan) over the top of the lasagne before serving.

NOTE If you don't have a fishmonger, the best way to acquire frozen shellfish is to ask at your local supermarket fish counter. Also, if you want to prepare the lasagne a few hours in advance, make the tomato mixture and béchamel while the fish is defrosting and make sure they are completely cold before assembling the lasagne.

SALMON IN CHAMPAGNE SAUCE
SERVES 6

Well, it doesn't have to be the real thing - a sparkling Saumur would be good - but either way it has a celebratory edge.

6 middle-cut skinless salmon fillets,
    each weighing approx. 150g
275ml champagne
20g butter, plus a little extra for
    greasing
2 medium shallots, finely chopped
20g plain flour
200ml double cream
1 x 50g jar salmon caviar, to garnish
a few sprigs of fresh dill, to garnish
seasoning

A large, lidded deep frying pan with
    a diameter of 25cm to hold the
    salmon fillets in one layer.

First of all, smear a little butter over the base of the frying pan, then arrange the fillets in it. Now slowly pour the champagne over the salmon (it will foam quite a lot, but not to worry), then bring it to a simmer over a medium heat. Next spoon the champagne over the top of the fillets before putting the lid on. Then gently poach the salmon for about 8–10 minutes. The tip of a knife inserted into the thickest part will show if it is cooked when you just ease the flesh back.

While the salmon is poaching, melt the butter in a medium saucepan and cook the shallots over a gentle heat for 5–6 minutes, until softened and golden but not browned. When the salmon is cooked, carefully lift the fillets on to a warmed dish (reserve the poaching liquid), cover them with foil and keep warm. Next, add the flour to the buttery shallot juices, stir it in and cook for 1–2 minutes more.

Now gradually add the salmon poaching liquid to the pan, a little at a time, then blend in the double cream, whisking until the sauce is smooth. Let it come to a simmer and cook for 1–2 minutes, then taste and add some seasoning.

Serve the salmon fillets on warmed plates with a little of the sauce spooned over, a teaspoon of salmon caviar and a sprig of dill on top, and hand the rest of the sauce around in a warmed jug. I think steamed Anya potatoes tossed in butter and chives are a nice accompaniment, and perhaps a green salad with plenty of cucumber and a lemony dressing.

HOT-SMOKED SALMON PIE
SERVES 4

This would be a good choice for Christmas Eve supper – done and dusted in the morning, or even the day before, then just whisked out of the fridge and into the oven. Imported fresh shelled peas involve no work and make an excellent accompaniment, as does steamed broccoli with a generous sprinkling of Parmesan.

2 x 160g packs hot-smoked salmon
   fillets
2 hard-boiled eggs (see page 89),
   peeled and roughly chopped
seasoning

FOR THE TOPPING
600g Desiree potatoes, peeled and cut
   into even-sized chunks
1 teaspoon salt
40g butter
2 tablespoons milk
1 tablespoon crème fraîche
25g Gruyère, grated
1 tablespoon freshly grated Parmesan

FOR THE SAUCE
275ml milk
20g butter
20g plain flour
cayenne pepper
25g grated Cheddar
1 tablespoon lemon juice
2 tablespoons crème fraîche
whole nutmeg, for grating
2 tablespoons chopped parsley
1 tablespoon capers, rinsed in cold
   water and patted dry
6 cornichons, roughly chopped

An 18cm square baking dish or similar
   and an electric whisk.

First steam the potatoes sprinkled with 1 teaspoon of salt for about 25 minutes, until they are absolutely tender, then drain off the water and return them to the saucepan and cover with a clean tea towel for 4 minutes. Then add the butter, milk and crème fraîche and use an electric whisk on slow speed to break up the potatoes then increase it to high and whip them up to a smooth, creamy, fluffy mass, then add some seasoning.

Meanwhile, make the sauce; place the first four ingredients into a small saucepan, set it over a gentle heat. Whisk continually until you have a smooth, glossy sauce, and simmer very gently for 5 minutes. Then add the rest of the ingredients. Whisk again and season.

Now preheat the oven to 200°C/gas mark 6.

Next take the skin off the salmon and break it into largish pieces, directly into the dish, then tuck the egg in among them. Pour the sauce over the salmon. Now spoon blobs of mashed potato, using a palette knife to spread it evenly over the surface and then make some indentations to form a pattern. Just run the palette knife in lines, pressing it down at 2.5cm intervals. Sprinkle the two cheeses all over the top, then place the dish on a baking tray and bake in the oven for 30–40 minutes, or until the surface is golden brown and the sauce underneath is bubbling.

Leave the pie to settle for 10 minutes out of the oven while you cook the vegetables to go with it.

HOT-SMOKED SALMON WITH A LEEK & MUSTARD CREAM SAUCE
SERVES 4

This not only tastes sublime, it's brilliantly easy. You can throw it all together any old time, keep it chilled and then pop it into the oven for 25 minutes whenever you need it. Spinach is a good accompaniment and creamy mash with capers added.

4 x 160g packs hot-smoked salmon fillets (weighing about 700g)
4 medium leeks, cleaned, halved and cut into thin slices
4 heaped tablespoons crème fraîche
6 tablespoons dry vermouth
1½ heaped dessertspoons grain mustard
a little butter
seasoning

A medium baking tray.

Preheat the oven to 180°C/gas mark 4.

Start off by laying a strip of foil lengthways over a baking tray (it has to be long enough to fold over to cover the salmon in a parcel), then lay a second strip across it at right angles. Butter the surface of the foil lightly, then arrange the chopped leeks over it and season them. Next remove the skin from the salmon pieces and arrange them on top of the leeks, seasoning them as well.

Now measure the crème fraîche into a bowl, add the vermouth and stir in the grain mustard. Pour this mixture all over the salmon and leeks, then bring the ends of the foil together over the salmon and squeeze them together to form an airy envelope around all the ingredients. Place the baking tray in the centre of the oven and cook for 20–25 minutes, until the leeks have cooked into the sauce (when opening the foil be careful not to let any of the precious sauce drain away). Then transfer the fish on to warmed plates and spoon the sauce over each one.

LUXURY SEAFOOD PIE WITH A PARMESAN CRUST

SERVES 6

The absence of high street fishmongers nowadays always poses problems, so it's important to point out that this recipe *can* be made using all frozen shellfish and any variety of white fish. However, what we recommend (because they are so good in December) is getting the scallops fresh. Likewise the fish, which can be monkfish, turbot or any firm white fish.

250g scallops (with corals if possible)
800g monkfish fillet, cut into 3cm
    pieces
250g frozen cooked mussels
250g frozen large, raw tiger prawns
450ml dry vermouth
1 bay leaf
FOR THE SAUCE
25g butter
15g flour
2 rounded tablespoons crème fraîche
1 heaped tablespoon fine capers in
    vinegar, drained, or salted capers,
    well rinsed
8 cornichons, drained and roughly
    chopped
1 heaped tablespoon chopped dill
a good pinch of cayenne pepper
seasoning
FOR THE PASTRY
375g ready-made butter puff pastry
20g freshly grated Parmesan, plus
    2 tablespoons to sprinkle
1 egg, beaten

A round pie dish 20.5cm in diameter
    at the base, 26cm at the top and
    3.5cm deep.

To start, if the scallops are large slice each one in half. Then pour the vermouth into a medium-sized saucepan and add the bay leaf. Bring it up to the boil, add the scallops and, when it comes back to a simmer, time it for exactly 1 minute before removing them with a draining spoon to a colander over a bowl. Next add the monkfish – in two batches – following the same procedure (back to a simmer, but this time cook each batch for 2 minutes). Next poach the frozen mussels (same as above, but remove them just as they come to a simmer) and finally the frozen prawns, only this time poach them until they turn pink and opaque. Then add the drained juices from the poached fish to the poaching liquid in the pan and bring it up to the boil, then reduce by two-thirds, which will take about 10 minutes. Then pour the poaching liquid into a jug, you need about 150ml.

Next make the sauce, do this by melting the butter in a small saucepan, stir in the flour, then gradually add the poaching liquid bit by bit, stirring continuously with a mini whisk. Cook on a gentle heat for 3–4 minutes, stirring occasionally. When the sauce has cooked, add the crème fraîche, capers, cornichons, and dill then season and add some cayenne pepper.

Once the sauce and fish are completely cold, mix them together in a bowl and pile into the pie dish.

Next roll the pastry to an oblong 20 x 30cm then use a pastry brush to dampen the surface with a little water and sprinkle evenly with the 20g of Parmesan, then fold the pastry over and roll it out to 35cm square. Now cut two 2cm strips from two of the edges of the pastry square. Dampen the rim of the dish with water, press the strips of pastry on to the rim and dampen them. Press the rest of the pastry loosely over that to form a lid and, using a sharp knife, trim any excess pastry off. Then press the edges firmly together and flute them all round. Make a steam hole in the centre with a skewer and roll any pastry trimmings together and cut them into leaves or little fish to decorate the top! Cover and chill for at least an hour, but it will be fine until the following day.

When you are ready to cook the pie, preheat the oven to 220°C/gas mark 7, then brush the pastry with beaten egg and sprinkle with the rest of the Parmesan. Place the pie on a baking tray and cook on the centre shelf of the oven for 25 minutes, then reduce the oven temperature to 180°C/gas mark 4 and cook for a further 20 minutes. Leave to stand for about 5 minutes before serving.

A VERY SPECIAL SEAFOOD RISOTTO
SERVES 4

Why special? Michael. He loves risotto in Italy and *soupe de poissons* in France, and this is a combination of the two, so for him it's heaven – me too.

1 x 400g pack frozen fruits de mer
275ml Arborio rice (as measured in a glass jug)
1 teaspoon butter
1 teaspoon olive oil
1 x 850g jar soupe de poissons
120ml dry white wine
1 tablespoon olive oil
1 large shallot, peeled and chopped

FOR THE SAUCE
1 teaspoon salt flakes
1 fat clove garlic
2 rounded teaspoons hot paprika (not smoked)
2 heaped tablespoons good-quality mayonnaise

TO SERVE
4 tablespoons grated Gruyère

A medium saucepan or flameproof casserole.

First, prepare the sauce by pounding the salt and garlic to a paste with a pestle and mortar, then stir in the paprika and mayonnaise and whisk it all together. Now, in the saucepan or casserole, heat the butter and 1 teaspoon of oil, then stir in the rice and, when it's all glistening and the grains are coated with butter and oil, pour in the soup and wine (no need to season). Give it all a good stir and turn the heat down so that everything simmers very gently (without a lid) for about 20 minutes, giving it a stir from time to time.

Meanwhile, heat 1 tablespoon of oil in a large frying pan and, when it's hot, add the shallot, cook for about 5 minutes, then add the fruits de mer straight from the freezer (stand back, as they will splutter as they go in). Keep the heat high and stir it all around for about 5 minutes, until the prawns have turned pink and opaque on both sides. Then transfer the whole lot to join the rice after the 20 minutes is up. Stir well and continue to cook for another 6 or so minutes, until the rice grains are tender but still have some bite. Serve the risotto in warmed bowls with the sauce and Gruyère separately.

BAKED HALIBUT WITH ENGLISH BUTTER SAUCE & SHRIMPS
SERVES 2

This is an exquisite sauce to serve with any fish, but was traditionally served with halibut. Although this recipe is enough for two, you can very easily make it for four or six (allowing an extra 5 minutes for the baking).

2 skinned fresh halibut fillets, each
    weighing about 200g
2 tablespoons dry vermouth
50g butter, chilled
2 x 57g pots Morecambe Bay potted
    brown shrimps
150ml water
1 tablespoon plain flour
1 dessertspoon lemon juice
1 teaspoon anchovy paste
a good pinch of ground mace
a good pinch of cayenne pepper
1 dessertspoon chopped parsley
seasoning

A small baking tray.

Preheat the oven to 180°C/gas mark 4.

To prepare the fish, place it on a small baking tray covered with a sheet of foil that will be large enough to wrap the fish, sprinkle over the vermouth and put a teaspoon of the butter on to each fillet, then season. Bring the edges of the foil over the fish and seal them together to form a parcel so that it is not touching the top of the fish. This can be done in advance if you keep it chilled. When you're ready, put the fish on the centre shelf of the oven and bake for 25–30 minutes.

To make the sauce: unmould the potted shrimps and ease the top layer of butter away from the shrimps. Keep the shrimps on one side and roughly dice the rest of the butter, as well as the shrimp butter. Next whisk the water and flour together in a small saucepan placed over a gentle heat and bring it up to simmering point, then add the lemon juice, anchovy paste, mace and cayenne.

Then, while it is still simmering, whisk in the butter – about three pieces at a time, adding more as it disappears into the sauce. When all the butter is in, add the shrimps and finish off by adding 2 tablespoons of the cooking juices when the fish comes out of the oven. Finally add the chopped parsley and some seasoning. Serve the halibut on warmed plates with the sauce spooned over.

A VEGETARIAN Christmas

I ADMIT THIS HAS always been a challenge at Christmas, and I have been guided here by veggie friends who follow my recipes and have given me some idea of what they're looking for. 'Something without the inevitable cheese' was one response (see page 169), and another was 'something that has "all the trimmings" like a traditional Christmas' (see page 167). I've enjoyed the challenge, but would like to add that where we have used a cheese that's not strictly vegetarian, a different option can be used (likewise a vegetarian gelatine can be used where required).

WATERCRESS & BUTTERMILK VICHYSSOISE
SERVES 8

You could serve this soup warm if you prefer, but I think a chilled soup is no different in winter from a cold starter and both have the advantage of being made well in advance.

350g watercress (reserve a few leaves for garnishing)
275ml buttermilk
110g butter
the white parts of 3 leeks (about 350g), washed and chopped
1 medium onion, chopped small
700g potatoes, peeled and chopped
1.75 litres vegetable stock (made with Marigold bouillon)
seasoning

A 3.5 litre lidded saucepan and a large bowl or plastic container.

First of all, melt the butter in the saucepan, then add the prepared leeks, onion, potatoes and half the watercress. Stir them around so that they're coated with the melted butter.

Next, sprinkle over some salt, then cover with a lid and let the vegetables sweat over a very gentle heat for about 20 minutes, giving the mixture a good stir about halfway through.

After that, add the stock, bring everything up to simmering point and simmer, covered, for about 10–15 minutes, or until the vegetables are quite tender. Then remove the pan from the heat and leave the soup to cool a little, and liquidise until it is smooth – a stick blender is useful here. Next, transfer to a large bowl or plastic container and leave until cold.

When the soup is cold, stir in three-quarters of the buttermilk and season to taste. Cover with clingfilm and chill thoroughly before serving – overnight is ideal. When you are ready to serve the soup, whiz the remaining watercress in a blender with about a third of the chilled soup (remembering to reserve a few leaves for garnishing) and when it is smooth, stir it into the rest of the soup.

Serve in bowls that have been very well chilled and garnish each one with a swirl of the remaining buttermilk and a few reserved watercress leaves.

ROASTED RED PEPPERS STUFFED WITH FENNEL
SERVES 4-6 AS A FIRST COURSE

Roasted peppers never fail to please and the fennel gives them an extra dimension. Don't forget to have lots of crusty bread to mop up the wonderful juices.

4 large red peppers
1 x 400g tin Italian plum tomatoes
2 small bulbs fennel
8 dessertspoons good-quality olive oil
1 rounded teaspoon mixed pepper
    berries
¾ teaspoon whole coriander seeds
½ teaspoon fennel seeds
salt flakes
the juice of ½ lemon

A large baking tray.

Preheat the oven to 180°C/gas mark 4.

Slice each pepper in half lengthways, cutting right through the green stalk and leaving it intact; though it won't be eaten, it adds much to the look of the thing. Remove all the seeds. Place the pepper halves on the baking tray, then drain the tomatoes (you don't need the juice) and divide them into eight equal portions, placing each portion inside a pepper half. Pare off any brownish bits of fennel with your sharpest knife and cut the bulbs first into quarters and then again into eighths, carefully keeping the layers attached to the root ends.

Now put the fennel in a saucepan with a little salt, pour boiling water on them and blanch them for 5 minutes. Then drain them in a colander and, as soon as they're cool enough to handle, arrange two slices in each pepper half. Sprinkle 1 dessertspoon olive oil over each one, using a brush to brush the oil round the edges and sides of the peppers.

Next lightly crush the pepper berries, coriander seeds and fennel seeds with a pestle and mortar or rolling pin and bowl, sprinkle these evenly all over the fennel and peppers, and finish off with some salt flakes. Then bake the peppers for approximately 1 hour on a high shelf in the oven until they are soft and the skin is wrinkled and nicely tinged with brown. After removing them from the oven, sprinkle the lemon juice all over and cool.
NOTE If you want to make the peppers ahead of time, cover with clingfilm after cooling, but don't refrigerate them as this spoils the fragrant flavour.

TOMATO TART WITH SWISS CHEESE & ROSEMARY
SERVES 6-8

This recipe was kindly given to me by a lady called Christiane who lives in Nice. You'd think that when they eat it there it would be made with fresh tomatoes ripened in the Provençal sun – but no, she uses tinned tomatoes, bought puffed pastry and frozen chopped onion! That said, it really is the best tomato tart we've ever tasted. And it doesn't end there, because it freezes very well and takes only 10 minutes to heat from frozen.

2 large onions, peeled and chopped, or
    250g frozen chopped onion
2 tablespoons olive oil
3 x 400g tins whole Italian tomatoes in
    tomato juice
1 bird's-eye chilli, deseeded and finely
    sliced
½ teaspoon sugar
2 cloves garlic, peeled and crushed
1 tablespoon finely chopped rosemary
200g ready-made butter puff pastry
1 tablespoon Dijon mustard
3 slices of Emmental
2 tablespoon extra virgin olive oil
seasoning

A porcelain tart dish or quiche tin with
    a base measurement of 22.5cm,
    lightly buttered, and a baking tray.

Begin by cooking the onions in 2 tablespoons of olive oil and some seasoning over a gentle heat in a medium-sized pan or casserole until soft and melting, which will take about 30 minutes. Meanwhile roughly chop the tomatoes and drain them really well in a sieve.

Now add the tomatoes, chilli, sugar, garlic and rosemary to the onions and cook over a gentle heat (stirring from time to time) until everything has reduced and become really thick. This will take about 45 minutes and at the end of the cooking time you should have no spare liquid in the pan, then remove the pan from the heat, cool and add some seasoning.

While the tomato filling cools, roll the pastry to a 28cm round and line the flan dish, pushing the pastry well into the edges, then trim away the pastry hanging over the side with a small sharp knife and prick the base. Now spread the mustard over the base using the back of the tablespoon and then cut each of the slices of Emmental into four and spread them out evenly across the base of the tart.

Preheat the oven to 200°C/gas mark 6 and place the baking tray in the oven. When the tomato filling has cooled, spread it evenly over the cheese and drizzle with 1 tablespoon of the extra virgin olive oil. Place it on the preheated baking tray and bake on the centre shelf for 30 minutes, until the pastry is crisp and deep golden brown. When it comes out of the oven, drizzle with the remaining oil and serve cut into wedges.

TO FREEZE When it's absolutely cold, wrap it in double foil. Then reheat on a baking tray at the same temperature for 10 minutes before serving.

CHEESE CHOUX PASTRIES FILLED WITH MUSHROOMS IN MADEIRA

SERVES 2

This one always goes on our Christmas party menu at the football club. It's very popular with vegetarians who want to feel they have had something really special at Christmas. You can make the filling and the raw choux pastry the day before.

FOR THE CHOUX PASTRY

150ml cold water

50g butter, cut into small pieces

60g strong plain flour

2 eggs, well beaten, plus extra to glaze

60g Gruyère, grated

½ teaspoon mustard powder

cayenne pepper

FOR THE FILLING

15g dried porcini mushrooms, soaked in 75ml boiling water for 30 minutes

40g butter

175g onions, finely chopped

2 cloves garlic, crushed

175g open-cap mushrooms, roughly chopped

175g oyster mushrooms, roughly chopped

½ teaspoon chopped fresh thyme

whole nutmeg

150ml Madeira

75ml double cream

seasoning

a few sprigs of watercress, to garnish

A good, solid baking sheet, lightly greased.

Preheat the oven to 200°C/gas mark 6.

To make the filling, melt the butter in a medium-sized saucepan and soften the chopped onions and garlic in it till pale gold (about 5 minutes). Then stir in all the fresh mushrooms and the soaked mushrooms, together with their soaking water. Season and add the thyme and a few good gratings of nutmeg. Now pour in the Madeira, cover and simmer gently for 1½ hours, making sure the liquid doesn't all evaporate.

To make the pastry you are going to need to 'shoot' the flour quickly, so fold a sheet of baking parchment to make a crease, then open it up again. Sift the flour straight on to the baking parchment and season it. Now place the water and butter in a saucepan over a moderate heat and stir with a wooden spoon. As soon as the butter has melted and the mixture comes up to the boil, turn the heat off immediately and tip the flour in (all in one go) with one hand while beating the mixture vigorously with the other (you can do this with a wooden spoon, but an electric hand whisk would be much easier).

Beat until you have a smooth ball of paste that has left the sides of the pan clean (probably less than 1 minute), then beat eggs in, a little at a time, mixing each addition in thoroughly before adding the next, until you have a smooth glossy paste. Then add 50g of the grated cheese, the mustard powder and a seasoning of salt and cayenne. Take heaped teaspoonfuls of the choux pastry and stack them closely together on the baking sheet to form two rings roughly 14cm in diameter. Brush each ring with beaten egg, then sprinkle them with the rest of the cheese.

Place them on a high shelf of the oven and bake for 10 minutes. After that raise the temperature to 220°C/gas mark 7 and continue baking for 20 minutes till crisp, then slit them in half horizontally. Stir the cream into the mushroom filling, then divide this between the two choux bottom halves. Place the other two halves on top, put a few sprigs of watercress in the centre of each for colour, and serve as soon as possible.

CHEESE & PARSNIP ROULADE WITH SAGE & ONION STUFFING

SERVES 4-6

This recipe was written some years ago, in response to a letter I received from a vegetarian who asked if I could devise something that had stuffing, sauce and all the trimmings, so that he could feel as Christmassy as everyone else. Well, here it is again – just as it was in the first book – in view of the appreciative response from vegetarians everywhere. All the trimmings could include Bread Sauce (see page 266) and Cranberry Relish (see page 261).

FOR THE ROULADE
40g butter
25g plain flour
275ml cold milk
3 eggs, separated
110g Cheddar, grated
1 rounded tablespoon chopped sage
40g hazelnuts, chopped and toasted
1 tablespoon grated Parmesan
seasoning

FOR THE STUFFING
40g butter
225g onions, chopped
1 heaped tablespoon chopped sage
1 tablespoon chopped parsley
75g white breadcrumbs
seasoning

FOR THE FILLING
350g parsnips (prepared weight)
25g butter
2 tablespoons double cream
whole nutmeg, for grating
seasoning

A Swiss roll tin 30 x 20cm, lined with
   baking parchment.

Preheat the oven to 200°C/gas mark 6.

First, make the stuffing by melting the butter in a small heavy-based saucepan, then add the onions and cook them for about 6 minutes, or until they are transparent. Next add the herbs, breadcrumbs and seasoning, stirring well to combine everything, and sprinkle the mixture evenly all over the lined tin.

Now for the roulade: place the butter, flour and milk in a saucepan and whisk them together over a medium heat until thickened, then season and leave the sauce to cook over the gentlest possible heat for 3 minutes. After that draw the pan off the heat to cool slightly, then add the egg yolks, whisking them in really well. Next add the grated cheese and sage, and taste to check the seasoning.

In a large bowl (and with a spanking-clean whisk) beat the egg whites until they form soft peaks. Gently fold a spoonful of the egg-white mixture into the cheese mixture – to loosen it – then spoon this mixture, a little at a time, into the rest of the egg white. Now spread the whole lot evenly into the prepared tin over the stuffing mixture and bake on the top shelf of the oven for 20-25 minutes, or until it feels springy and firm in the centre.

Meanwhile, cook the parsnips in a steamer for 10-15 minutes, until they're soft, then cream them together with the butter, double cream and some seasoning and nutmeg (this can be done by hand or in a food processor). When they're ready, keep them warm while you lay a sheet of baking parchment (slightly longer than the roulade) on a work surface and sprinkle the hazelnuts all over it.

When the roulade is cooked, turn it out on to the hazelnuts and carefully peel off the base paper. Spread the creamed parsnip evenly all over the sage and onion stuffing. Now, with the shortest end of the roulade nearest you, roll the roulade away from you, using the parchment to help you (it's not difficult, it behaves very well). Transfer the roulade to a serving plate and sprinkle the surface with a dusting of grated Parmesan.

NOTE This can be made ahead and reheated from chilled for 40 minutes at 200°C/gas mark 6. Remove the foil for the last 10 minutes to brown the top.

A LUXURIANT VEGETABLE PIE
SERVES 6

The challenge here was to find a celebration recipe for vegetarians without any cheese. After several attempts, this one emerged as the clear winner.

400g ready-made butter shortcrust
    pastry
1 small egg, beaten (to glaze)
FOR THE FILLING
400g fennel
275g leeks
200g tenderstem broccoli
175g frozen baby broad beans
100g pine nuts, toasted
1 heaped tablespoon fine capers,
    drained
12 cornichons, roughly chopped
FOR THE SAUCE
40g butter
55g plain flour
650ml vegetable stock (made with
    Marigold bouillon)
150ml double cream
75g watercress, stalks removed, plus
    extra for garnish
seasoning

A large lidded pan and a fan steamer
    or a steamer, a loose-based non-
    stick sandwich tin with a base
    measurement of 20cm and 4cm
    deep, lightly greased, and a baking
    tray.

To start, prepare the vegetables; trim away a little of the stalk from the fennel, cut it in half through the root, then into 1cm slices. Trim the leeks, keeping just a little of the dark green part, then slit them vertically to about halfway down and fan them out under the tap to remove any grit. Then cut diagonally into 1.5 cm slices. Trim away a small piece off the base of each broccoli stalk, then cut it into pieces about 6cm long.

Next, set a fan steamer over boiling water and first put in the fennel to one side, cover with the lid and set the timer for 1 minute then place the leeks next to the fennel and set the timer for 1 more minute followed by the broccoli next to the leeks for 2 minutes and finally, add the broad beans and steam for a further 2 minutes, by which time all the vegetables should be al dente and still retain their colour. Then remove them from the steamer into a large bowl to cool.

Preheat the oven to 200°C/gas mark 6 with the baking tray.

To make the sauce, melt the 40g of butter in a medium saucepan then stir in the flour and gradually whisk in the stock. Bring it up to a simmer, then cook very gently for 4–5 minutes. After that, remove from the heat and stir in the two-thirds of the cream and some seasoning. While the sauce cools, roll a little over half the pastry to a 28cm round on a floured surface (giving it quarter-turns to form the round), then line the sandwich tin, pushing it well into the edges and leaving the overhang for the moment.

Now take the cooled sauce and whiz the watercress into it either with a stick blender or a processor until the sauce is green but still has some flecks of watercress in it. Put a quarter of the sauce into the bowl with the cooked vegetables and reserve the remaining sauce in a cool place for later. Now add the toasted pine nuts, capers and cornichons to the vegetables and gently give it all a thorough mix to coat everything lightly, adding a little more sauce if necessary. Have a taste now and add more seasoning if necessary before piling it into the lined pastry.

Now roll the remaining pastry 3mm thick and 24cm wide and dampen the edges of the base and lay the lid on the top. Pinch the base and the lid well together where they overlap the tin, then use a pair of scissors to trim away the excess pastry, leaving a 1.5cm overhang. Fold in the overhang using your thumb and forefinger to form a scalloped edge. Roll and cut some leaves with the pastry trimmings and use them to decorate the top. Brush all over with the egg glaze and use a skewer to make a hole in the centre for the steam to escape. If you want to make this in advance refrigerate and leave the glaze until later.

Put the pie on the hot baking tray and bake for 40 minutes.

When the pie comes out of the oven, leave it to stand for about 5 minutes. Heat the sauce in a medium saucepan without boiling and, when it is hot, whisk in the last 15g of butter and 50ml cream before removing from the heat and pouring into a warmed jug.

Carefully remove the pie from the tin, then serve whole or cut into wedges on warmed plates with the hot sauce and some extra watercress to garnish if you like.

CHEDDAR, SAGE & ONION 'SAUSAGE' ROLLS
MAKES 36

These were originally called Vegetarian 'Sausage' Rolls, but they're so good we've changed the name so that everyone can enjoy them.

1 quantity of quick flaky pastry (see page 86) or 400g ready-made butter puff pastry
beaten egg, to seal and glaze
FOR THE FILLING
275g fresh breadcrumbs
225g mature Cheddar, grated
1 large onion, grated
3 tablespoons thick double cream
3 tablespoons chopped sage
1½ teaspoons mustard powder
a pinch of cayenne pepper
seasoning

Three baking sheets, lightly greased.

Preheat the oven to 220°C/gas mark 7.

For the filling, simply place all the ingredients in a mixing bowl and mix very thoroughly. Then form the mixture into three and roll each into a 35cm long sausage shape. Place them on a tray and cover and chill for about 30 minutes. Meanwhile, roll the pastry on a lightly floured surface to a rectangle measuring 50 x 40cm, then trim it to 45 x 35cm to give nice neat edges and cut three oblongs measuring 15 x 35cm.

Place a roll of the cheese mixture on one strip of pastry. Brush the beaten egg along one long edge, then fold the pastry over and seal it as carefully as possible. Lift the whole thing up and turn it so the sealed edge is underneath. Press lightly and cut diagonally to make 12 even-sized 'sausage rolls'. Snip three V shapes in the top of each roll with the end of some scissors and brush with beaten egg.

Repeat with the other pieces of pastry and cheese mixture, then divide between the greased baking sheets and bake in the oven for 20–25 minutes, swapping the trays around as the top ones will brown more quickly. Then leave them to cool on a wire rack before storing in an airtight tin (that's if they're not all eaten before you get a chance!).

These freeze well and can be warmed through in the oven.

A STILTON & LANCASHIRE CHEESE TERRINE WITH SPICED PEAR CONFIT

SERVES 8 AS A FIRST COURSE

A wonderful combination here, which would also make a light lunch for four people, served with a green leaf salad and some crusty bread.

110g Stilton, crumbled

110g Lancashire cheese, crumbled

275g cottage cheese

7g leaf gelatine (or sufficient vegetarian gelling agent to set 570ml of liquid)

75g mayonnaise

1 dessertspoon lemon juice

150ml double cream

3 tablespoons snipped fresh chives

seasoning

watercress, to serve

FOR THE SPICED PEAR CONFIT

5-6 small, hard pears with stalks

1 tablespoon lemon juice

500ml dry cider

100ml cider vinegar

1½ tablespoons soft dark brown sugar

1 teaspoon allspice berries

½ teaspoon cloves

½ teaspoon black peppercorns

1 cinnamon stick

A 450g loaf tin measuring 15 x 9.5 x 7cm, lightly oiled with groundnut oil.

Start by putting all the ingredients for the pears (except the pears and lemon juice) in a medium-sized pan and bring it slowly up to simmering point. Meanwhile, peel the pears and brush them with lemon juice then take each pear and lay it on a chopping board with the stalk against the board and, with a small, sharp knife, cut through the stalk first, then stand the pear up and split it in half. Now lay the halves cut-side down on the board and again cut through the stalk first, then split the pear into quarters.

Cut out the cores and put the pears into the simmering liquid, turn the heat down very low and cook for 1 hour without a lid, turning them every now and then. After an hour test the pears to make sure they are tender, then transfer them (with a draining spoon) to a dish. Then boil the liquid for about 5 minutes to reduce it to a sticky syrup and pour this over the pears. When they are cool, cover and refrigerate till needed.

To make the terrine, start off by dealing with the gelatine. Put the leaves into plenty of cold water and soak for 5 minutes (longer wouldn't hurt). Then in a processor blend the cottage cheese, mayonnaise and lemon juice together until absolutely smooth. Next whip up the double cream until it has thickened to the floppy stage, but be careful as it should not be too thick.

Now remove the gelatine leaves from the water, squeeze them out and put them in a small saucepan. Melt over a gentle heat – it will only take about 30 seconds to become liquid. Once it has melted, remove from the heat and pour into the cottage cheese mixture with the machine running. Then tip this mixture into a large bowl and add the crumbled cheeses, chives and seasoning. Finally, fold in the cream and turn the whole lot into the prepared tin. This should be done quite speedily, before it begins to set. Cover with clingfilm and chill in the fridge for several hours till firmly set.

To turn out the terrine, carefully slide a palette knife around the edge of the tin, invert on to a serving plate and give the base a sharp tap. Serve in slices with the pears and some watercress.

MACADAMIA & PISTACHIO NUT ROAST WITH SPICED YOGHURT SAUCE
SERVES 6

This recipe is specially for my friend Lilie, who is a vegetarian and said I couldn't possibly not include a nut roast. So here it is and can be served hot with the sauce or cold with pickles and chutneys.

300g salted, roasted mixed nuts
1 tablespoon coriander seeds
1 tablespoon cumin seeds
2 tablespoons groundnut oil
300g onions, finely chopped
1 large green pepper, deseeded and
    chopped
15g jalapeño pepper, drained and
    chopped
2 large cloves garlic, crushed
75g shelled pistachios
50g wholemeal breadcrumbs
2 heaped tablespoons chopped
    coriander
1 x 400g Italian plum tomatoes
2 eggs, beaten
seasoning
FOR THE TOPPING
10g butter, melted
40g macadamia nuts, roughly chopped
40g pistachios, roughly chopped
FOR THE SAUCE
400g Greek strained yoghurt
½ teaspoon coriander seeds
½ teaspoon cumin seeds
the seeds from 3 fresh cardamom pods
1½ teaspoons turmeric
¼ teaspoon ground cinnamon
¼ teaspoon salt flakes

A loose-base sandwich tin, 20 x 4cm,
    well buttered, and a baking tray.

Start this off on the day before you need it. Using a pestle and mortar, crush together the coriander and cumin seeds (for the roast), then warm a small frying pan over a medium heat and add the crushed spices. Turn up the heat high and toss them around to dry-roast them and draw out the flavour (which will take about a minute) then tip them into a bowl and leave on one side.

Now crush and dry-roast the whole spices for the sauce in the same way, then put them in a small mixing bowl to cool. Then into the bowl stir the yoghurt, turmeric, cinnamon, coriander and some seasoning. Cover and leave in a cool place (or fridge) for several hours or overnight for the flavour and colour to develop.

When you want to cook the nut roast, preheat the oven to 200°C/gas mark 6, take a medium-sized frying pan, heat the oil and cook the onions for a few minutes before adding the green and jalapeño peppers, garlic and all but ½ teaspoon of the prepared spices and cook for about 10 minutes, until everything has softened. Meanwhile, chop the mixed nuts fairly small by hand, or carefully pulse them in a processor. Then drain the tomatoes and chop them. Now, in a large bowl, mix together the roasted chopped nuts, pistachios, breadcrumbs, fresh coriander and tomatoes, then add the cooked onion mixture and season well before adding the eggs.

Now pile the mixture into the prepared tin and press down well, then drizzle with the melted butter and sprinkle with the chopped macadamia and pistachio nuts. Bake for 35 minutes. Serve the nut roast cut into wedges with the spiced yoghurt in a separate bowl sprinkled with the reserved crushed spices.

PAPPARDELLE PIE WITH WILD MUSHROOMS & TALEGGIO
SERVES 6

This is exquisite and pappardelle which are wide flat ribbons work well but any dried pasta can be used.

300g pappardelle (wide egg pasta ribbons)
15g dried porcini mushrooms
150ml Marsala wine
2 tablespoons olive oil, plus extra for drizzling
1 medium onion
400g large chestnut mushrooms
250g large, dark-gilled mushrooms
6 cloves garlic
570ml milk
50g butter
40g flour
½ whole nutmeg, freshly grated
2 tablespoons double cream
150g Taleggio, cut in cubes
40g grated Parmesan
seasoning

A large, wide, shallow pan and a 20 x 28 x 5cm baking dish, well buttered.

Begin by placing the porcini (broken into pieces) in a small saucepan, add the Marsala, bring up to simmering point, then take it off the heat and put on a timer for the porcini to soak for 30 minutes.

Meanwhile, peel and chop the onion and the same with the garlic. Then heat 2 tablespoons of olive oil in a wide shallow pan, add the onions and let them cook over a lowish heat for about 10 minutes. While that's happening, chop the chestnut mushrooms (through the stalk) into quarters and the larger mushrooms into six. After that add the garlic to the onion and cook, stirring it around, for a minute or two before adding the prepared fresh mushrooms.

Stir and toss them around until they start to shrink, add some seasoning and let them cook very gently. Then, when the 30 minutes' soaking time is up, add the porcini and Marsala and do some more tossing and stirring. Continue to cook with the heat at medium for about 30–40 minutes, or until all the juices (of which there will be quite a lot) have evaporated. It could take a bit longer, but this will concentrate the flavour of the mushrooms beautifully. Put a large pan of water on to boil and preheat the oven to 200°C/gas mark 6.

Meanwhile, make an all-in-one béchamel sauce by placing the milk, butter and flour in a saucepan, then whisking over a medium heat until you have a smooth, thick sauce. Then turn the heat to its lowest and cook for 5 minutes, adding some seasoning and the nutmeg. At the end whisk in 2 tablespoons of double cream.

When the mushrooms are ready, cook the pasta in the boiling water for 8 minutes, then drain it in a colander. Return it to the saucepan, add two-thirds of the sauce, along with the mushrooms and cubes of Taleggio. Now pile the whole lot into the gratin dish, cover the pasta with the rest of the sauce and finally sprinkle with the Parmesan and drizzle with a little olive oil.

Bake in a preheated oven for 20 minutes until golden brown. This can all be prepared in advance, but in that case it will need 30–40 minutes in the oven. Either way, when it is removed from the oven, allow it to settle for 10 minutes before serving on hot pasta dishes.

ORECCHIETTE WITH WALNUT SAUCE
SERVES 2

So simple but so, so good is how best to introduce this recipe. It is a great standby for serving to unexpected guests who don't eat fish or meat. I've used orecchiette ('little ears') here, but any small pasta shapes will do. It's very rich, so it would be good to serve it with a simple salad made with some crisp chicory and a lemony dressing.

175g orecchiette pasta
75g shelled walnuts
2 cloves garlic, peeled
4 tablespoons mascarpone
2 heaped tablespoons freshly grated
   Parmesan, plus extra to serve
seasoning

Begin by chopping half the walnuts finely together with the garlic in a mini-chopper or small processor. Then combine this mixture in a bowl with the mascarpone and Parmesan, and add some seasoning.

Now bring a pan containing 2 litres of salted water to the boil and warm two pasta bowls. Add the pasta to the water, give it one good stir and let it simmer for about 12 minutes. Meanwhile, chop the rest of the walnuts (not too finely this time).

Drain the pasta in a colander, return it to the pan and quickly stir in the walnut sauce, keeping the pan over a low heat as you do so to warm the sauce through. Serve the pasta with the rest of the nuts sprinkled over and some more Parmesan at the table.

VEGETABLES
in Winter

WITH VEGETABLES IT IS always better to try to follow the seasons – fresh British vegetables are always going to be the best (and cheapest). This is particularly true at Christmas, and that's what I've confined this chapter to. You could argue that so good are they – tiny Brussels sprouts, red and green cabbage, celery, leeks and all the root vegetables – that recipes as such are not strictly needed. What follows is really a little embellishment here and there, but basically keeping it simple.

MICHAEL'S CHUNKY SAUTÉ POTATOES IN TURKEY DRIPPING
SERVES 4-6

This is a once-a-year special treat for us – Michael's crisp, crunchy sauté potatoes. The secret, he says, is cooking them in one layer – and they are absolutely scrummy with slices of cold bacon (or gammon) and turkey, with pickles and chutneys.

900g Desiree potatoes
2 tablespoons turkey dripping (or goose fat)
salt flakes

Two medium, heavy-based frying pans and a warmed serving dish.

Peel the potatoes to start with and, if any of them are particularly big, slice them in half. Now par-boil them in salted water for 8–10 minutes before draining them and cutting them into 1cm chunks or slices. Next, divide the dripping equally between the 2 frying pans and heat till smoking hot, then add the chunks or slices of potatoes in one layer. Turn the heat down to medium and cook them for about 10 minutes on one side, then flip them over, one by one, and cook for approximately the same time. They should be golden and crispy on the outside and soft in the centre. Remove to some kitchen paper, to get rid of any excess fat, and then to the serving dish, lined with crumpled baking parchment. Sprinkle them with salt flakes before you send them to the table.

ROASTED ROOTS WITH HERBS
SERVES 4

This is a winner for entertaining, not least because all the vegetables can be cooked together with little or no attention. This can also be prepared 2–3 days before, tossed in oil and herbs and kept in a polythene bag in the fridge.

4 small whole carrots
4 small whole parsnips
150g swede, cut into 2.5cm wedges
1 small turnip, cut in half and then into
    2cm slices
2 medium red onions, peeled and cut
    through the root into quarters
2 red potatoes, unpeeled, about 150g
    each, cut into 6 wedges
1 fat clove garlic, crushed
3 tablespoons olive oil
1 tablespoon chopped mixed herbs
    (including thyme, rosemary
    and sage)
seasoning

A large solid baking tray.

Preheat the oven to 240°C/gas mark 9.

First scrub the carrots and parsnips, dry them well and place them in a large bowl with all the other prepared vegetables. Now add the crushed garlic, olive oil and mixed herbs, then, using your hands, mix well to make sure they all have a good coating of the oil. You can leave them like this, covered with clingfilm, for up to 2 hours until you are ready to cook them – in which case the oil will have nicely absorbed the flavour of the garlic and herbs.

Then arrange them on the baking tray, season and cook in the preheated oven on a high shelf for 35–40 minutes, or until they are cooked through.

JACKET POTATO WEDGES WITH MELTING CHEESE & SPRING ONION

SERVES 4

Good old jacket potatoes, no peeling and sitting happily in the oven. Then cut into wedges and flashed under the grill with cheese, a great way to serve potatoes in winter.

700g small potatoes, washed
50g mature Cheddar, grated
4 spring onions, chopped small
    (including the green parts)
olive oil
salt flakes

A medium-sized solid, shallow roasting
    tin, a grill pan and some foil.

Preheat the oven to 180°C/gas mark 4.

First rub each potato with olive oil and sprinkle generously with salt. Bake them on a high shelf in the oven for an hour. Then preheat the grill for 10 minutes, cut each potato into quarters and place them in a grill pan lined with foil. Scatter the spring onions over the potatoes, then sprinkle on the grated cheese. Place under the grill until the cheese has browned and is bubbling.

PURÉE OF POTATO & CELERIAC WITH GARLIC
SERVES 8

This is a beautiful combination of flavours and perfect, as all purées are, for serving with braised dishes that have lots of sauce. Because you don't want to be mashing potatoes at the point when your guests are just arriving, we tested this, making it a couple of hours in advance and keeping it warm. There were no ill-effects whatsoever.

1kg celeriac
450g potatoes
2 fat cloves garlic, peeled
50g butter
150ml double cream or crème fraîche
seasoning

A large heatproof mixing bowl.

First tackle the celeriac. You will need to have a bowl of cold water ready in which to put the prepared pieces to prevent it browning. Peel the celeriac thickly with a knife. Then cut into approximately 2cm cubes. Leave these pieces in the water whilst preparing the potatoes. Peel and cut these into 2.5cm cubes – i.e. slightly larger than the celeriac. Now place the prepared vegetables in separate saucepans with 1 clove of garlic to each saucepan. Pour enough boiling water over the vegetables just to cover them, add salt and simmer them for about 10 minutes, or until they are tender.

Drain each vegetable in a colander, place them together in a large heatproof mixing bowl and add the butter and cream or crème fraîche, and some seasoning. Next, using an electric hand whisk, whisk them to a purée using the slow speed to break them up, then the fast one to whisk them till smooth. Now taste and season the purée, then place the bowl in a roasting tin half-filled with barely simmering water and it will keep warm quite happily until your guests arrive.

POTATOES BOULANGÈRE WITH SAGE
SERVES 8

Potatoes boulangère – so named because French bakers would offer to bake people's potatoes in their ovens after the bread was baked – are crisp and golden on the top, soft and creamy within. They are perfect for entertaining, as they sit happily in the oven without needing any attention.

1.15 kg Desiree potatoes, peeled
2 medium onions
1 heaped tablespoon finely chopped
    sage, plus 8 small sage leaves
275ml vegetable stock (made with
    Marigold bouillon)
150ml milk
40g butter
a little olive oil, for dipping
seasoning

An ovenproof dish 28 x 20cm and
    5cm deep, lightly buttered.

Preheat the oven to 180°C/gas mark 4.

Begin by peeling and cutting the onions in half and then the halves into the thinnest slices possible; the potatoes should be sliced, but not too thinly (about 3mm thick). Now all you do is arrange a layer of potatoes, then onions, in the dish, followed by a scattering of chopped sage then season. Continue layering in this way, alternating the potatoes and onions and finishing with a layer of potatoes that slightly overlap.

Now mix the stock and milk together and pour it over the potatoes and put little flecks of butter all over the top. Then place the dish on the highest shelf of the oven for 1 hour, by which time the top will be crisp and golden and the underneath creamy and tender. Ten minutes before the end of the cooking time dip the sage leaves in a small dish of olive oil and scatter them over the top of the potatoes.

NOTE If you want to prepare this well ahead, cook for 30 minutes and then for another 30 minutes or so before serving.

ALL-IN-ONE BAKED VEGETABLES
SERVES 4

What this one avoids is your having to run backwards and forwards to the kitchen on Christmas morning to see if the vegetables are done. This recipe allows you to sit down and sip your pre-lunch champagne without moving. Also, because the vegetables are baked in a foil parcel, there's absolutely no washing up!

350g carrots, scrubbed and cut into
    2.5cm chunks
350g parsnips, scrubbed and cut into
    5cm chunks
350g small red potatoes, unpeeled,
    each cut into 8 wedges
1 medium red onion, peeled and cut
    into 8, through the root
1 head celery, trimmed and cut into
    8cm chunks
5 tablespoons vinaigrette dressing
2 sprigs thyme
2 sprigs rosemary
1 bay leaf
seasoning

A 35 x 28cm and 2cm deep roasting
    tray and a 90 x 30cm sheet of foil.

Preheat the oven to 200°C/gas mark 6.

All you do is fold the piece of foil in half, then lay one half along the length of the roasting tray, brush it with a little of the vinaigrette, and lay all the vegetables on the foil on the tray. Season them well.

Add the sprigs of herbs and the bay leaf, then spoon the remaining vinaigrette over and toss all the vegetables around so they get a good coating – you'll need to do this quite carefully so as not to break the foil. Now fold over the other half of the foil and turn over all the edges 2 or 3 times to seal it all round. What you should end up with is a parcel that fits the tray exactly but with some air space between the foil and vegetables.

When you're ready to cook the vegetables, place them in the preheated oven, one shelf higher than the middle, for 45 minutes.

To serve, carefully unwrap the foil and tip the vegetables into a warm serving dish.

BRUSSELS BUBBLE-AND-SQUEAK
SERVES 4

In theory this should be made with leftover sprouts, and at any other time it is, but at Christmas we never seem to have enough left over, so we just cook some more. The more crusty and brown it goes the better we like it. Then all it needs are slices of turkey and ham and some chutney and pickles.

350g Brussels sprouts, cooked
450g Desiree potatoes, cooked, then
    mashed with butter and milk
1 tablespoon turkey dripping
seasoning

A medium-sized, heavy frying pan.

Chop the sprouts quite finely and combine them with the mashed potato, seasoning well. Now take a medium frying pan and melt the turkey dripping in it over a high heat. When it's really hot, pile in the potato mixture, using a palette knife to spread it all over the base of the pan and patting it down quite firmly. Then turn the heat down to medium. What you're aiming at here is a lovely crisp golden crust, which will take about 7 minutes on the first side. Then place a plate on top of the frying pan and, using a cloth to protect your hand, invert it, turning the pan over so the bubble and squeak settles on the plate. Now put the pan back on the heat and use a palette knife to slide and gently ease the mixture back into the pan to brown on the other side for about 5 minutes. Serve the bubble-and-squeak cut into thick wedges with cold cuts.

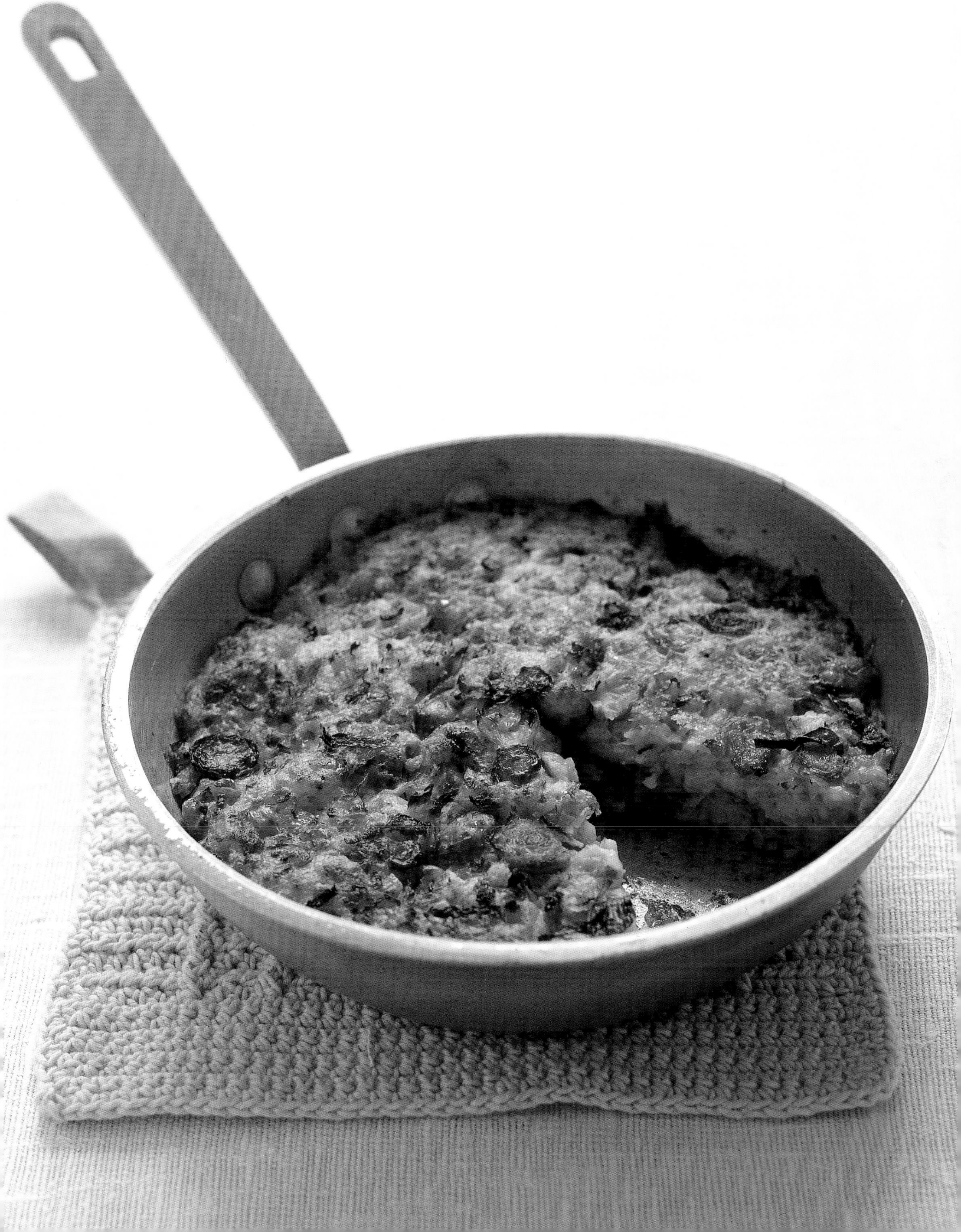

GRATIN OF CELERY WITH STILTON
SERVES 2

This can be served either as an accompanying vegetable, or I actually think it is nice enough to serve as a vegetarian main course with some nutty brown rice.

225g celery stalks
50g Stilton
2 heaped tablespoons half-fat crème fraîche
2 heaped tablespoons breadcrumbs
1 dessertspoon butter, melted
celery salt
seasoning

A small gratin dish, 15 x 15cm or similar, lightly buttered.

Preheat the oven to 200°C/gas mark 6.

Start off by trimming the celery stalks and cutting them into 13–15cm lengths so they fit snugly into the gratin dish. Then peel them to get rid of the stringy bits, pop them into a steamer and steam for just 7 minutes.

Now arrange the celery over the base of the gratin dish and add some seasoning. Crumble the Stilton all over the celery, tucking it into any gaps as well, then spoon the crème fraîche over, using a spatula to spread it evenly all over the surface.

Finally, toss the breadcrumbs in the melted butter then sprinkle them evenly over the top and give them a light sprinkling of celery salt. Then transfer the dish to the centre of the preheated oven and cook for 25 minutes, until the top has browned nicely and the celery stalks are tender.

PARSNIPS WITH PARMESAN
SERVES 8

This is one of the nicest ways to serve parsnips, baked crisp and golden brown in the oven with a Parmesan coating. They can be prepared well in advance, up to 24 hours, or they can even be prepared and frozen and will then cook perfectly if allowed to defrost first.

1.25kg parsnips
50g freshly grated Parmesan
175g plain flour
groundnut or other flavourless oil, for
    baking
a knob of butter
seasoning

A large solid roasting tin.

Begin by combining the flour, Parmesan and some seasoning in a mixing bowl. Peel the parsnips using a potato peeler. Then halve and quarter them lengthways and cut each length in half across, so that you end up with smallish chunks. Cut out any tough woody centres. Now pop the parsnips in a saucepan, pour in enough boiling water just to cover them and add salt. Put on a lid, bring them to the boil and boil for 3 minutes.

Meanwhile, have a large kitchen tray ready. Then, as soon as they are ready, drain them in a colander and, whilst they are still steaming, drop a few at a time (with the aid of some kitchen tongs) into the flour and Parmesan mixture, shaking the bowl and moving them around so that they get a good even coating. As they are coated, transfer them to the tray. Make sure you do them all fairly swiftly as the flour mixture will only coat them whilst they are still steamy! When they're all coated they are ready to cook or cool and store in the fridge or freeze.

When you're ready to bake them, preheat the oven to 200°C/gas mark 6 and pop the roasting tin with the butter and oil in to preheat as well. Then, when the oven is ready, remove the tin and place it over direct heat (turned fairly low) and, again using tongs, place the parsnips quickly side by side in the tin. Tilt it and baste all the parsnips with hot fat, place the tin back in the oven and bake them for 20 minutes, then turn them over, drain off any surplus fat and continue to bake for a further 15–20 minutes, or until they are crisp and golden.

TRADITIONAL BRAISED RED CABBAGE WITH APPLES

SERVES 10–12 PEOPLE

This is a recipe I have been cooking for years. It's great because it can be made a day or two before and gently reheated with no last-minute bother. It is a perfect accompaniment to venison, goose or pork (and if you have any left over it does wonders for bangers and mash).

1kg red cabbage
450g onions, chopped small
450g cooking apples, peeled, cored
 and chopped small
1 clove garlic, chopped very small
¼ whole nutmeg, freshly grated
¼ teaspoon ground cinnamon
¼ teaspoon ground cloves
3 tablespoons brown sugar
3 tablespoons wine vinegar
15g butter
seasoning

A large casserole with a tight-fitting lid.

Preheat the oven to 150°C/gas mark 2.

First, discard the tough outer leaves of the cabbage, cut it into quarters and remove the hard stalk. Then shred the rest of the cabbage finely, using your sharpest knife (although you can shred it in a food processor, I prefer to do it by hand because it doesn't come out so uniform). Next, in a fairly large casserole, arrange a layer of shredded cabbage and some seasoning, then a layer of chopped onions and apples with a sprinkling of garlic, spices and sugar. Continue with these alternate layers until everything is in.

Now pour in the wine vinegar and lastly add dots of butter on the top. Put a tight lid on the casserole and let it cook very slowly in the oven for 2–2½ hours, stirring everything around once or twice during the cooking. Red cabbage, once cooked, will keep warm without coming to any harm and it will also reheat very successfully. And yes, it does freeze well, so all in all, it's a real winner of a recipe.

SAUTÉED CARAMELISED FENNEL
SERVES 4–6

Fennel's lovely aniseed flavour is here warmed up by caramelising with sugar and cider vinegar. Traditionally fennel goes with fish but this recipe is also recommended with roast meats.

4 medium fennel bulbs
25g butter
1 rounded teaspoon granulated sugar
275ml medium cider
55ml cider vinegar
salt

A wide (24cm in diameter) saucepan with a lid into which the trimmed fennel will fit snugly and a fan steamer.

To prepare the fennel bulbs, first cut off the leafy fronds and reserve them for a garnish. Then slice off the root part at the other end, keeping the bulb intact, and remove any tough or brown outer layers, then slice across each bulb to cut it in half. Next place the fennel in a fan steamer set in the saucepan with 2.5cm of boiling water. Cover and steam for 10 minutes, then remove the fennel from the steamer, throw out the water, wipe the inside of the saucepan with absorbent kitchen paper and return it to the heat.

Then melt the butter and sugar in the saucepan and when it starts to foam, stir it around the pan until the sugar dissolves, then add the fennel, cut side down. Keeping the heat fairly high, brown it for 5 minutes, then turn the pieces over and brown them on the other side for another 3 minutes.

Now combine the cider, cider vinegar and a little salt, and pour this into the pan, then keeping the cut side of the fennel facing upwards, cover with a lid and simmer gently for 20 minutes. After that turn the fennel over again. Then continue to cook for a further 20–25 minutes (this time uncovered). Watch carefully during the last 10 minutes and test to see if it is cooked by inserting a skewer.

When the fennel is tender enough, raise the heat so that the remaining juices reduce to a glaze. Shake the pan carefully to give an even covering of the caramel glaze. Now transfer the whole lot to a warm serving dish with the cut surfaces upwards and scatter with the fennel fronds as a garnish.

SAUTÉED BRUSSELS SPROUTS WITH CHESTNUTS

SERVES 4

This is a long-standing Christmas favourite and I love the brown and caramelised edges of the sprouts and the sweetness of the chestnuts.

275g baby Brussels sprouts
200g frozen peeled chestnuts,
    defrosted (or vac-packed)
8 shallots or 1 small onion
40g butter
seasoning

A large frying pan.

First, put a medium pan of water on to boil. Blanch the Brussels sprouts for 30 seconds and drain them well. Now, peel the shallots (or peel the onion and finely chop it, in a mini chopper if you have one). Now heat the butter in a large frying pan and, when it's foaming, add the shallots or onion and fry for 2 minutes over medium heat until slightly softened. Next, add the Brussels sprouts and some seasoning.

Then cook for about 6–8 minutes, stirring them around, until the shallots or onion and Brussels sprouts are looking slightly brown and caramelised and are cooked through. Lastly, add the chestnuts to the pan and cook for a further 3–4 minutes until the chestnuts are hot, then pile everything into a warm serving dish.

SALT-CRUSTED MINI BAKED POTATOES WITH COLD CHIVE HOLLANDAISE
SERVES 10

This is top drawer for a party or a buffet supper. The recipe has been in print for 19 years and never fails to please.

20 small red potatoes (approximately jumbo-egg size)
olive oil
1 tablespoon salt flakes
FOR THE HOLLANDAISE
6 egg yolks
4 tablespoons lemon juice
2 tablespoons white wine vinegar
350g butter
seasoning
25g chives, snipped

First of all, make the hollandaise by placing the egg yolks in a small bowl and season them. Then place them in a food processor or blender and blend them thoroughly for about 1 minute. After that heat the lemon juice and vinegar in a small saucepan until the mixture starts to bubble and simmer. Switch the processor or blender on again and pour the hot liquid on to the egg yolks in a slow, steady stream. After that switch the processor or blender off. Now, using the same saucepan, melt the butter over a gentle heat, being very careful not to let it brown. When the butter is foaming, switch the processor or blender on once more and pour in the butter in a thin, slow, steady trickle; the slower you add it the better. (If it helps you to use a jug rather than pouring it from the saucepan, warm a jug with boiling water, discard the boiling water and pour the butter mixture into that first). When all the butter has been incorporated, wipe around the sides of the processor bowl or blender with a spatula to incorporate all the sauce, then give the sauce one more quick burst and you should end up with a lovely smooth, thick, buttery sauce. Then pour it into a bowl and stir in two-thirds of the snipped chives. Cover the bowl with clingfilm and leave in the fridge until the sauce is cold and set.

Next scrub the potatoes thoroughly and dry them with a tea towel, then leave them aside for the skins to dry completely (if you get ready-scrubbed potatoes, just wipe them with damp kitchen paper).

Preheat the oven to 190°C/gas mark 5.

When the skins are nice and dry, prick them with a fork, then moisten your hands with oil and rub the potatoes to oil them all over. Put the tablespoon of salt flakes in a bowl and swirl each potato in the salt to coat it lightly.

Place the potatoes on a baking sheet and bake for 1 hour, or until crisp and tender. Then when you're ready to serve, cut a cross in the top of each potato and gently squeeze up from the base to open out the cut slightly (use a towel to protect your hands). Arrange the potatoes together on a large warmed serving dish and quickly top each one with a spoonful of the chive hollandaise then sprinkle with the reserved chives.

If you like a lighter sauce you can use foaming hollandaise (see page 291).

The SWEETEST *Christmas*

THIS IS, ADMITTEDLY, A rather large chapter, but
then restraint is not the order of the day at Christmas.
Happiness is forgetting self-denial for a few days and
enjoying all the luscious sweets, puddings and desserts
on offer without guilt. We are celebrating, are we not?
There's a lot here, but that's because each one of them
was too good to leave out!

CRANBERRY JELLIES WITH FROSTED CRANBERRIES

SERVES 4

We always have to have this one once over the Christmas period. It's cool and light, and looks very bright and festive.

570ml cranberry juice

the juice and zest of 2 oranges

9g leaf gelatine (5 sheets measuring about 11 x 7.5cm each)

½ teaspoon powdered ginger

1 cinnamon stick, broken into pieces

75g caster sugar

FOR THE FROSTED CRANBERRIES

approximately 24 cranberries

1 egg white, beaten

1 tablespoon caster sugar

Four 200ml glasses.

First place the gelatine leaves in cold water and leave them to soften. Next take a potato peeler to pare off the outer zest of the oranges and put the zest in a saucepan with the cranberry juice, orange juice, ginger, cinnamon and sugar. Bring everything up to a gentle simmer, then remove from the heat. Now squeeze out the excess liquid from the soaked gelatine, whisk it into the hot liquid and leave to stand for 2 hours, until the jelly is just on the point of setting. Now strain the jelly through a nylon sieve into a jug to remove the zest and cinnamon, pour into glasses, cover and chill in the fridge until needed.

For the frosted cranberries all you need to do is dip each berry into beaten egg white and roll it in caster sugar to give a generous coating. Then leave the berries spread out on baking parchment to become crisp.

Remove the jellies from the fridge 30 minutes before serving and pile some frosted cranberries on top of each glass.

NOTE If you prefer you can make the jelly in a 725ml jelly mould, turn it out and decorate it with the cranberries.

PETITS MONTS BLANCS
SERVES 8

If you have time to make your own meringues they do freeze well (see deliaonline.com), but you can now buy some very good-quality meringue nests, and in that case you have a recipe that takes only moments.

8 ready-made meringue nests
2 x 250g tins crème de marrons
   (sweetened chestnut purée), chilled
250g mascarpone, chilled
1 teaspoon pure vanilla extract
200g fromage frais (8% fat), chilled
1 rounded dessertspoon golden caster
   sugar
8 whole marrons glacés, sliced
a little sifted icing sugar

Eight star-shaped sparklers (see
   page 15).

Make the mascarpone vanilla cream by whisking the mascarpone, vanilla extract, fromage frais and caster sugar together and chill till needed. To assemble the Monts Blancs, spoon equal quantities of the crème de marrons into each meringue and then spoon the mascarpone cream on top. Add some sliced marrons glacés to each one and dust with icing sugar, adding a sparkler to each one to light at the table if you like.

CHESTNUT FLOATING ISLANDS
SERVES 6

This is cool and light – as are traditional floating islands – and the chestnuts add a Christmas dimension. Microwaving the meringues is a breeze, but if you don't have a microwave you can poach the meringues in simmering water in heaped tablespoonfuls, giving them 1 minute each side and drain them on kitchen paper.

3 egg whites
40g golden caster sugar
1 x 250g tin crème de marrons
    (sweetened chestnut purée)
300ml single cream
6 marrons glacés

Six sundae glasses or shallow
    glass bowls and six teacups.

In a clean, grease-free bowl whisk the egg whites until they form stiff peaks, then gradually whisk in the sugar till you have a stiff glossy mixture. Spoon the meringue into six teacups. Then, three at a time, place the cups in the microwave and cook on a medium setting for 1 minute 45 seconds, until they have risen and are slightly firm to touch. The meringues will shrink back down as they cool then keep them covered still in the cups in the fridge until you are ready to serve.

To make the sauce, simply whisk together the chestnut purée and the cream, then chill really well. Finally, cut the marrons glacés into small pieces.

To serve, divide three-quarters of the sauce between the glasses, then spoon a meringue on to each one (don't tip them out, as some liquid may have gathered in the base of the teacup). Lastly drizzle a little sauce over each one and sprinkle with the marrons glacés.

SPICED CRANBERRY & ORANGE BRÛLÉE
SERVES 4

An easy, unctuous and very Christmassy do-ahead dessert. You can use a cook's blowtorch for the brûlée, but the caramel won't be as crunchy as putting it under the grill.

400g cranberries
the grated zest of 1 large navel orange
75g golden caster sugar
1 teaspoon ground ginger
½ teaspoon ground cloves
½ teaspoon ground cinnamon
250g Greek yoghurt
200ml crème fraîche
175g demerara sugar

A heatproof dish, 23 x 15 x 5cm,
    or similar.

Preheat the oven to 180°C/gas mark 4.

Place the cranberries in the dish and add the orange zest. Sprinkle with the caster sugar, followed by the spices, give everything a good stir and pop the dish in the oven. Cook for 40–45 minutes until the cranberries have started to collapse and the juices have almost evaporated, then leave them to cool completely.

Meanwhile, combine the yoghurt and crème fraîche in a bowl and when the cranberries are cold spread this mixture over evenly, making sure it goes right up to the edges. Cover with clingfilm and put in the fridge for at least 1 hour.

When you're ready to make the topping, preheat the grill to its highest setting – do let it heat up for at least 10 minutes. Sprinkle the demerara evenly over the crème fraîche and yoghurt, then place the dish about 7.5cm from the grill and let it bubble and turn a lovely golden-brown colour – this should take about 8 minutes, but watch it like a hawk. Leave it to cool, then place in the fridge, uncovered, until you want to serve it. It will keep crunchy for up to 4 hours.

CHAMPAGNE JELLIES WITH SYLLABUB
and Frosted Grapes
MAKES 6

Sparkling, cool jellies with a special touch of class. No, it doesn't have to be champagne; in fact, a sparkling Saumur works very well. It's nice served in champagne glasses, or wine glasses, placed on a small tray in the fridge to stop them toppling over.

FOR THE JELLY
275ml champagne or medium-dry sparkling white wine, very well chilled
1 large lemon
85g caster sugar
10g leaf gelatine

FOR THE SYLLABUB
1 tablespoon champagne or medium-dry sparkling white wine
½ tablespoon brandy
1 tablespoon lemon juice
10g caster sugar
75ml double cream

To make the jelly, pour 450ml water into a saucepan. Next pare the zest of the lemon using a peeler. Add this to the pan, together with the sugar, and bring up to simmering point. Meanwhile, soak the gelatine leaves in cold water for 5 minutes to soften. Then take the pan off the heat. Squeeze the excess water from the gelatine and whisk it into the mixture. Next add the juice of the lemon and strain the contents of the pan into a large bowl. Leave to cool, cover and chill in the fridge until the jelly is just on the point of setting – this should take 1–1½ hours, but keep an eye on it. Then give it a really good whisk.

After that uncork the champagne, measure out 275ml and pour it into the jelly. Stir once or twice to blend everything, then ladle gently into the serving glasses (being gentle means trying to conserve as many bubbles as you can). Chill the jellies, covered with clingfilm, for 4 hours, by which time they should have a deliciously soft set, not rubbery but firm enough to support the syllabub.

Make the syllabub by combining the champagne, brandy, lemon juice and sugar in a bowl. Leave this on one side, stirring occasionally, until the sugar has dissolved. Then pour in the cream and whisk until it stands in soft peaks; cover and chill until you are ready to serve. Just before serving, top each jelly with blobs of the syllabub cream and decorate with frosted grapes.

FROSTED GRAPES

110–150g seedless white grapes
1 egg white, beaten
caster sugar

For the best effect try to separate the grapes into clusters of two or three depending on their size, leaving them still attached to the stalk. Then wash and dry them thoroughly and dip them first into the egg white and then into the sugar, making sure each one gets an even coating of sugar. Spread them out on baking parchment to dry for a couple of hours before using to decorate.

TRADITIONAL ENGLISH TRIFLE
SERVES 6-8

This one's the real deal. Though we love making trifles all the year round, we only ever make this one at Christmas – which keeps it in the very special occasion bracket. We have discovered that frozen English raspberries are better than imported fresh ones at Christmas time, and that bog-standard trifle sponges absorb Madeira better than home-made.

FOR THE CUSTARD
4 egg yolks
25g golden caster sugar
1 dessertspoon cornflour
425ml whipping cream
1 teaspoon pure vanilla extract
FOR THE FILLING
6 trifle sponges
2 tablespoons seedless raspberry jam
150ml Sercial Madeira (or dry sherry)
275g frozen raspberries
1 dessertspoon golden caster sugar
2 medium-sized bananas
FOR THE TOPPING
275ml whipping cream
50g toasted flaked almonds

A 1.75 litre glass bowl.

It's best to start this with the filling, so slice the sponges in half lengthways, spread one half with jam and place the original half back on top. Cut each one into three mini sandwiches and place these sideways up in the bowl (they should all fit into a single layer). Now stab them with a small knife and carefully and slowly pour the Madeira over all of them. Then leave on one side so the sponges absorb the liquid - tip the bowl from time to time to make sure there are no pools of liquid in the bowl.

Now make the custard. First whisk the cornflour, egg yolks and sugar together in a bowl. Then heat the cream in a small saucepan and, when it comes up to simmering point, pour it on to the egg mixture, whisking as you pour. Now quickly pour the whole lot back into the saucepan, add the vanilla and whisk over a medium heat until it just begins to bubble and thicken (don't worry, it won't curdle - if it does look at all grainy, it will become smooth again when whisked off the heat). Pour it back into the bowl and leave to cool.

The raspberries should be placed in a saucepan straight from the freezer, together with the sugar. Then cook them over a gentle heat, stirring them around only until they have collapsed and defrosted and the juices start to run. This will take about 5 minutes, then let them cool.

To assemble the trifle, tip the bowl from side to side to make sure all the Madeira has soaked into the sponges, then peel and slice the bananas. Strain off any excess juice from the raspberries. Then scatter them over the sponges, followed by the bananas. Now pour the custard all over. Finally, whip the cream till thick, spoon it over and spread it around, and scatter the almonds all over. Cover the bowl with clingfilm and chill until needed.

PANETTONE & ZABAGLIONE TRIFLE
SERVES 6-8

The trouble with a really good panettone is that whenever I use it I can't help sneaking a slice every time I go into the larder. It's quite unique and special. It makes not only one of the best steamed puddings (see page 53) but also this outstanding trifle.

150g panettone
75g organic dried apricots, cut into 4
75g raisins
200ml Marsala wine
FOR THE CUSTARD AND
TOPPING
5 egg yolks
1 tablespoon caster sugar
1 dessertspoon cornflour
150ml Marsala wine
600ml double cream
50g toasted flaked almonds

A 1.75 litre glass bowl.

First of all, put the apricots and raisins in a small saucepan with 150ml of the Marsala. Bring up to simmering point, then take off the heat and leave to soak for 40 minutes. Meanwhile, cut the panettone into slices about 2cm thick, then cut these down to about 4cm pieces and place them in the bowl.

After that strain the cooled soaked fruit over a jug and add enough Marsala to make the liquid up to 150ml. Then sprinkle the Marsala evenly over the panettone, followed by the fruit. Leave to one side so the panettone can soak up all the juices, and tip the bowl from time to time to make sure there are no little pools of liquid in the bowl.

To make the custard, whisk the egg yolks, sugar and cornflour in a medium bowl. Then place 350ml of the cream and the Marsala in a saucepan and, over a gentle heat, bring up to simmering point, then, whisking the egg mixture all of the time with one hand, gradually pour the hot cream back into the bowl with the egg mixture. Now quickly pour the whole lot back to the saucepan, using a rubber spatula. Whisk over a medium heat until it just begins to bubble and thicken (don't worry, it won't curdle – if it does look at all grainy, it will become smooth again when whisked off the heat).

Let the custard get quite cold then pour it over the fruit and panettone. Then whip the remaining cream to the floppy stage (being careful not to make it too stiff) and spoon it all over the custard. Cover and chill till needed, sprinkling over the toasted almonds just before serving.

CHOCOLATE CHESTNUT LOG
SERVES 6–8

This is a must-have Christmas dessert that never fails to please. I have been making various versions for 40 years, but this is now established as our favourite at Christmas.

6 eggs, separated
150g golden caster sugar
50g cocoa powder, sifted
FOR THE CHOCOLATE MOUSSE
110g dark chocolate (70–75%
    cocoa solids), broken into
    small pieces
50ml warm water
1 egg, separated
10g golden caster sugar
150ml double cream
1 x 250g tin crème de marrons
    (sweetened chestnut purée)
a little icing sugar, sifted

A tin 30 x 20 x 2.5cm, oiled and
    the base lined with baking
    parchment.

Begin by making the chocolate mousse filling. Place the chocolate and the warm water in a medium heatproof bowl and sit over a saucepan containing 5cm of barely simmering water, without the bowl touching the water – it will take 5–10 minutes to become melted and glossy. Then remove the bowl from the pan and stir the chocolate briskly till it is smooth and then let it cool for a few minutes. After that beat in the egg yolk with a wooden spoon.

In a spanking clean bowl, whisk the egg white to the soft-peak stage, then whisk in the sugar so the mixture is glossy. Next stir 1 tablespoon of the egg white into the chocolate and fold in the rest. Place the bowl covered with clingfilm in the fridge for about 30 minutes to firm up.

Now preheat the oven to 180°C/gas mark 4 and you can get on with the cake: place the egg yolks in a large bowl and whisk until they start to thicken, then add the caster sugar and whisk until the mixture thickens slightly and finally whisk in the cocoa powder. In another spanking-clean bowl, whisk the egg whites with a clean whisk to the soft-peak stage, then carefully cut and fold the egg whites into the chocolate mixture about a third at a time. Now pour the whole lot into the prepared tin and cook in the centre of the oven for 20–25 minutes until springy and puffy.

Leave the cake to cool in the tin (it will shrink a bit, but that's normal), then when it is cold, turn it out on to a piece of baking parchment that has been generously dusted with icing sugar. Peel off the lining parchment from the bottom of the cake (which is now facing upwards), then gently spread the chilled chocolate mousse all over it using a palette knife. Next empty the chestnut purée into a bowl, add a tablespoon of the double cream and mix thoroughly before spreading it over the chocolate mixture, again using a palette knife. Lastly, whip the rest of the double cream until it is just firm but still smooth and is holding its shape, and spread that all over.

Now, with the shortest end of the cake nearest you, roll the cake away from you, using the parchment to help you – if it cracks a little that will only add to the authenticity! Make sure the roll is sitting on the join, then wrap the parchment around it to help keep its shape and chill in the fridge for at least 1 hour (it will be fine for several hours in the fridge).

When you are ready to serve, transfer it to a serving dish, dust with icing sugar and finish with a sprig of holly if you like.

CHOCOLATE & SOUR CHERRY CRUMBLE

SERVES 6

If you are a chocolate lover – or a crumble lover – this is a truly sublime combination of the two. It's rich, luscious and perfect for a celebration. Serve it warm with vanilla ice cream, crème fraîche or my own favourite, chilled pouring cream.

125g sweetened sour cherries

75ml brandy

FOR THE CUSTARD BASE

570ml double cream

75g cocoa powder

5 egg yolks

50g caster sugar

1 dessertspoon cornflour

FOR THE CRUMBLE

40g cold butter, diced

60g self-raising flour

3 tablespoons cocoa powder

50g demerara sugar

75g whole almonds (skin on is OK)

TO FINISH

cocoa powder

1 tablespoon edible red or gold
    iridescent sugar sparkles

A 1 litre baking dish.

Begin by putting the cherries and brandy in a small saucepan and bring it just up to simmering point, then turn off the heat and leave them to soak and plump up for about 1 hour.

Meanwhile, whisk the cream and cocoa together in a medium-sized saucepan until blended and smooth then place it over a medium heat, bring it up to simmering point, then reduce the heat and simmer very gently for 10 minutes.

Now, in a medium bowl whisk together the egg yolks, sugar and cornflour, then (still whisking) pour the hot chocolate cream over the yolks. When it is all in, immediately return the mixture to the saucepan and, over a gentle heat, whisk again until it just reaches simmering point and has thickened (don't worry, it won't curdle – if it does look at all grainy, it will become smooth again when whisked off the heat). When it's ready, stir in the soaked cherries and any brandy, pour the whole lot into a baking dish and leave to cool completely.

While it's cooling make the crumble. Place the butter, flour, cocoa and sugar in a processor and give it a whiz until it resembles fine breadcrumbs, then add the almonds and process again (not too fast) until they are fairly finely chopped but still have a few chunky bits. If you don't have a processor, in a large bowl rub the butter into the sifted flour until it resembles breadcrumbs, then stir in the cocoa, sugar and almonds (which should be fairly finely chopped by hand).

Preheat the oven to 180°C/gas mark 4. Now sprinkle the crumble on to the cold chocolate custard, pressing it down lightly. Bake on the centre shelf of the oven for 35 minutes. When it's cooked, take it out and leave it to stand for 10 minutes. Serve dusted with cocoa powder and you can, if you like, sprinkle with sugar sparkles.

COCONUT & LIME CHEESECAKE WITH A CONFIT OF LIMES

SERVES 4-6

Coconut and lime makes a great partnership, and the sharp, fragrant confit here cuts through the rich creaminess of the cheesecake. Make the confit well in advance, as it really needs steeping overnight.

FOR THE BASE

40g coconut biscuits, crushed

20g Grape-Nuts

10g toasted flaked almonds

25g melted butter

FOR THE CHEESECAKE

200g limes, juiced and zest grated

25g desiccated coconut

3g leaf gelatine (2 leaves measuring 11 x 7.5 cm each)

50g creamed coconut (block)

175g ricotta

1 egg yolk

30g caster sugar

4 tablespoons milk

125ml double cream, whipped to the floppy stage

FOR THE CONFIT OF LIMES

3 large limes, thinly sliced, plus juice of 1 lime

110g granulated sugar

340ml water

A 15cm loose-based cake tin, lined with baking parchment, a small baking tray and a medium non-aluminium saucepan for the confit.

Preheat the oven to 200°C/gas mark 6.

Start by placing the lime for the confit in the saucepan and add cold water to just cover and simmer for 3 minutes, then drain and discard the water. Now pour 340ml water into the same pan, add the sugar and stir over a gentle heat until all of the grains have dissolved, then add the lime slices. Place a circle of baking parchment on the surface of the liquid and simmer gently without a lid for 35–40 minutes until tender. Then remove them with a draining spoon to a shallow dish. Now boil the remaining liquid to reduce it to 150ml. Add the lime juice, then pour over the sliced limes, cool and chill in the fridge.

To make the cheesecake, begin by tipping the base ingredients into a bowl and stir in the melted butter. Then press the mixture firmly onto the base of the tin and then pre-bake on the baking tray for 20 minutes, then leave to cool.

Then measure out 75ml of the lime juice into a jug, then stir the desiccated coconut into this and leave to soak for 10 minutes. Put the leaves of gelatine into a small bowl of cold water to soften. Next put the creamed coconut into a small saucepan and warm gently.

Now put the ricotta, egg yolk and sugar into a food processor and blend it all on a high speed for about 1 minute. Then add the milk to the coconut in the pan, stir together well and remove from the heat. Squeeze the excess water from the gelatine, then add it to the hot coconut mixture and stir until dissolved. Blend this into the mixture in the food processor. Next add the lime zest, desiccated coconut and any lime juice that hasn't been soaked up to the mixture in the processor and pulse a few times before finally adding the cream and blend for a few seconds, then pour the whole lot over the biscuit base, cover with foil and chill for at least 3 hours.

To serve the cheesecake, carefully remove from the tin, peel away all the baking parchment and put it on a serving dish. Slice with a clean sharp knife, then top each portion with a few lime slices and some syrup from the confit and hand the remaining confit and syrup round separately.

MAPLE WALNUT CHEESECAKE WITH CARAMELISED WALNUTS
SERVES 8

Pure Canadian maple syrup and walnuts have a great affinity – and if you caramelise the walnuts with the syrup the flavour is superb. Try to get Dark Amber No. 2 (or at least the darkest you can find) and you'll need two bottles, because one is not enough for this recipe.

250g walnuts, chopped
500ml maple syrup (1½ bottles)
110g rustic oat biscuits
40g melted butter
400g curd cheese
200g fromage frais (8% fat)
3 eggs, beaten

A 20cm springform cake tin, lightly buttered, base lined with baking parchment, and a baking tray.

Preheat the oven to 200°C/gas mark 6.

First combine the walnuts with 4 tablespoons of the maple syrup, tossing them around to coat them evenly. Then spread them out on a baking tray lined with baking parchment and bake on the centre shelf of the oven for 20 minutes, so they are nicely browned and caramelised. Then remove from the oven and let them cool.

To make the biscuit base, put 75g of the cooled caramelised nuts into a food processor, then add the biscuits and give a few pulses until chopped but not too finely. Now empty these into a bowl, mix well with the melted butter and press the mixture on to the base of the cake tin and bake it for 10 minutes. Remove it then reduce the temperature to 150°C/gas mark 2.

While the base cools a little, take 110g of the caramelised nuts and this time grind them in a food processor or mini-chopper until they are very finely chopped. Then, in a bowl, beat the curd cheese with 4 tablespoons of the maple syrup before mixing in the fromage frais, beaten eggs and finally the finely chopped walnuts. Now pour the filling evenly over the base and bake for exactly 30 minutes before turning the oven off, then leave it in the oven for 1½–2 hours to cool. After that, take it out and let it cool completely before covering with foil and chilling for at least 4 hours, or overnight is better.

To serve the cheesecake, slide a palette knife all round, then release the spring-clip and remove the side of the tin before carefully sliding the cheesecake from the base on to a serving plate, using the palette knife to help ease it off the base. Cover with the remaining walnuts and serve cut into wedges with extra maple syrup and some pouring cream.

NOTE We have found a variety of walnut called Serr which is extremely good quality, but they come in halves so you need to chop them roughly.

THE FAMOUS CHOCOLATE TRUFFLE TORTE
SERVES 10

Yes, this is the one where the nation ran out of liquid glucose, because of (it has to be admitted) the power of television. It has been much copied over the years, but the original is still the best and I'm still grateful to my friend, and chef, Derek Fuller, who gave me the recipe.

450g dark chocolate (70-75% cocoa solids)
5 tablespoons liquid glucose
5 tablespoons rum
570ml double cream, at room temperature
75g amaretti biscuits, crushed finely with a rolling pin
TO SERVE
cocoa powder
chilled pouring cream
some extra amaretti biscuits

A 23cm cake tin, lined with a circle of baking parchment and the base and sides lightly brushed with groundnut oil.

Start off by sprinkling the crushed biscuits all over the base of the tin. Next break the chocolate into sections and put them in a heatproof bowl together with the liquid glucose and the rum. Sit over a saucepan containing 5cm of barely simmering water, without the bowl touching the water – it will take 5-10 minutes to become melted, smooth and glossy. Stir, then take off the heat and leave the mixture to cool for 5 minutes or so, until it feels just warm.

Now, in a separate bowl, beat the cream to the floppy stage. Fold half into the chocolate mixture and then fold that mixture into the rest of the cream. When it is smoothly blended, spoon it into the prepared tin. Tap the tin gently to even the mixture out, cover with clingfilm and chill overnight.

Just before serving, run a palette knife round the edge to loosen the torte, then give it a good shake and turn the whole thing out on to a serving plate (don't be nervous about this – it's very well behaved). To serve, dust the surface with sifted cocoa powder and a few amaretti biscuits and, if you like, mark the top into serving sections. Have some chilled pouring cream to go with it; if you have any, a couple of tablespoons of amaretti liqueur will make a wonderful addition to the cream.

NOTE The torte does freeze well, but since you can also make it a couple of days in advance, this doesn't really seem necessary.

FALLEN CHOCOLATE SOUFFLÉ WITH ARMAGNAC PRUNES
SERVES 6–8

I make no apologies for including this recipe from *The Winter Collection*. Everyone loves it, and they deserve it at Christmas!

FOR THE SOUFFLÉ
200g dark chocolate (70–75% cocoa solids)
110g unsalted butter
1 tablespoon Armagnac
4 eggs, separated
110g golden caster sugar
a little sifted icing sugar or cocoa, for dusting

FOR THE ARMAGNAC PRUNES
350g Agen no-soak prunes
150ml Armagnac

FOR THE PRUNE AND CRÈME FRAÎCHE SAUCE
the remainder of the soaked prunes
150ml crème fraîche

A 20cm springform cake tin, greased and lined with baking parchment.

The prunes need to be soaked overnight, so simply place them in a saucepan with 150ml water, bring them up to simmering point remove from the heat then pour the prunes and their cooking liquid into a bowl and stir in the Armagnac while they're still warm. Leave to cool, then cover the bowl with clingfilm and chill in the fridge overnight.

To make the soufflé, preheat the oven to 170°C/gas mark 3. Meanwhile, break the chocolate into squares and place them with the butter in a bowl. Sit over a saucepan containing 5cm of barely simmering water, without the bowl touching the water – it will take 5–10 minutes to become melted, smooth and glossy. Now remove the bowl from the heat, add the Armagnac and leave to cool.

Next take a large roomy bowl and combine the egg yolks and caster sugar in it. Then whisk them together for about 5 or 6 minutes, using an electric hand whisk – when you lift up the whisk and the mixture drops off making ribbon-like trails, it's ready. Now count out 18 of the soaked prunes, cut each one in half and combine the halves with the whisked egg mixture along with the melted chocolate. Next you'll need to wash the whisk thoroughly with hot soapy water to remove all the grease, and dry it well.

In another bowl, whisk up the egg whites till they form soft peaks. After that, fold them carefully into the chocolate mixture. Spoon this mixture into the prepared tin and bake the soufflé in the centre of the oven for about 30 minutes, or until the centre feels springy to the touch.

Allow the soufflé to cool in the tin (it's great fun watching it fall very slowly but don't worry if it doesn't). When it's quite cold, remove it from the tin, peel off the paper, then cover and chill for several hours (or it can be made 2 or 3 days ahead if more convenient).

To make the sauce, simply liquidise the prunes reserved from above, together with their liquid. Place the purée in the serving bowl and lightly stir in the crème fraîche to give a slightly marbled effect. Serve the soufflé dusted with icing sugar or cocoa and cut into small slices (it's very rich). Hand the sauce round separately.

NOTE The prunes soaked in Armagnac and served with crème fraiche make an extremely good dessert in their own right. Also the soufflé and sauce freeze very well for up to a month.

FROZEN CHOCOLATE & VANILLA CRÈME BRÛLÉES
SERVES 6

The idea here is that the brûlées are still frozen in the centre. There are actually three layers, one vanilla, one chocolate and one caramel, and they are an absolute wow. Make them the day before so they have time to freeze or well ahead so you have a prepared dessert for any time over the holiday.

600ml double cream
6 egg yolks
1 tablespoon cornflour
2 tablespoons golden caster sugar
a few drops of pure vanilla extract
75g dark chocolate (70–75% cocoa solids), finely chopped
FOR THE CARAMEL
110g granulated sugar

Six ramekins with a base measurement of 7.5cm and a small solid baking tray.

First of all heat the cream in a medium-sized saucepan until it reaches boiling point and while it's heating, blend the yolks, cornflour and caster sugar in a bowl. Then pour the hot cream in, stirring all the time with a wooden spoon, and return the mixture to the saucepan.

Heat very gently, still stirring, until the custard has thickened – which should only take a minute or so (don't worry, it won't curdle – if it does look at all grainy, it will become smooth again when whisked off the heat). Now pour 350ml of the custard into a heatproof glass jug and add the vanilla extract. Stir the chopped chocolate into the remaining custard in the saucepan. Divide the chocolate custard between the six ramekins and use the back of a spoon to smooth the surface, then pour the vanilla custard on top. Leave to cool then cover with clingfilm and chill for 2 hours.

After that, preheat the grill to its highest setting for at least 10 minutes and make sure that when you put the ramekins on the grill pan they will be about 4cm from the heat source. Unwrap the crèmes and sprinkle them with the granulated sugar, giving them a gentle shake so the sugar is level. Place them on the baking tray, then put them under the hot grill for 4–5 minutes, until the sugar has melted and started to go very dark brown in some places. Now leave them to cool, then cover and freeze them for at least 3 hours or longer. Remove them from the freezer for 15 minutes before surprising your guests!

ICED CHOCOLATE CHESTNUT TORTE
SERVES 6-8

In the first book this was made in little pots, but I think the version below is a great improvement – not so much fiddle and much easier to gauge how long it's out of the freezer before you serve it. Either way it remains one of my top desserts of all time.

75g dark chocolate (70-75% cocoa
   solids)
1 tablespoon dark rum
2 eggs
2 x 250g tins crème de marrons
   (sweetened chestnut purée)
150ml double cream
FOR THE SAUCE AND TOPPING
275ml single cream
50g good-quality white chocolate,
   chopped
6 marrons glacés, cut into 5mm pieces
a dusting of icing sugar

A 20cm springform cake tin, base
   lightly oiled and base lined
   with baking parchment.

What happens here is that you make three layers and to begin the first one break up the dark chocolate and place it in a small basin, adding the rum. Then sit over a saucepan containing 5cm of barely simmering water, without the bowl touching the water – it will take 5-10 minutes to become melted, smooth and glossy. .

Meanwhile, separate the eggs, placing the yolks in one basin, but the whites in two separate medium-sized basins. As soon as the chocolate has melted, remove it from the heat and beat in the egg yolks. Next whisk one of the egg whites to the soft-peak stage, then carefully fold it into the chocolate mixture. Transfer this mixture into the prepared tin, smooth the surface with the back of a spoon, and pop it in the freezer while you make the centre layer.

Two bowls are needed here, one containing the contents of a tin of crème de marrons, the other the cream. First, whisk the cream to the floppy stage, then, using the same beaters, give the crème de marrons a quick whisk to soften it. After that fold the whipped cream into the crème de marrons until all the marbling has disappeared and it's thoroughly combined.

Next wash the whisk in warm soapy water to remove all traces of grease, dry it then whisk the other egg white until it reaches the soft-peak stage. Fold it into the cream mixture, pour that over the chocolate base, smooth the surface with the back of a spoon and continue to freeze for 1 hour. When the hour's up, whip the contents of the second tin of crème de marrons and spoon this on top. Cover with clingfilm and that's it – you can freeze it till you need it.

To make the sauce gently heat half of the cream in a small saucepan. When it's just hot enough to hold your finger in it, remove from the heat, add the chopped white chocolate and stir until it has melted, then add the remaining cream. Cool and chill in the fridge. Take the torte out of the freezer 35 minutes before you want to serve it. Remove the base parchment and put the torte on a serving dish. Cover with the chopped marrons glacés and place in the fridge for about 30 minutes, by which time you will be able to slice it with a sharp knife (it will be soft on the outside and semi-frozen in the middle). Dust with icing sugar and serve in slices with the sauce poured over.

PRUNE & ARMAGNAC ICE CREAM
SERVES 6

Home-made ice cream is in a different league from anything you can buy, and it means you've always got a dessert tucked away in the freezer. Instead of trying to think of presents for all the family why not get a consensus to buy an ice cream maker – a good investment that will last for years and bring so much pleasure.

500g no-soak prunes
275g double cream
275ml single cream
4 egg yolks
1 dessertspoon cornflour
110g golden caster sugar
2 tablespoons Armagnac

A food processor and an ice-cream
maker (pre-frozen according to
the manufacturer's instructions)
or an electric whisk.

First place 350g of the prunes in a medium-sized saucepan and add 425ml of cold water. Bring this up to simmering point, cover and simmer gently for 20 minutes, then leave to cool.

Now whip the double cream until it reaches the floppy stage but isn't too thick then pop it into the fridge to chill.

Next make a custard – first pour the single cream into a medium saucepan, then carefully heat it to just below boiling point. Meanwhile, beat together the egg yolks, cornflour and caster sugar in a bowl until absolutely smooth. Next pour the hot cream on to this mixture, whisking as you pour. Now return the custard to the pan and continue to whisk over a medium heat until it has thickened and come to just below boiling point again (don't worry, it won't curdle – if it does look at all grainy, it will become smooth again when whisked off the heat).

Rinse out the bowl and pour in the custard into it. Then place it in another larger bowl of cold water with a few ice cubes, stirring it now and then until it is absolutely cold.

While the custard is cooling, drain off the cooking liquid from the prunes and purée them in a food processor with the Armagnac until very smooth. Now roughly chop the remaining prunes into 5mm pieces. When the custard is completely cold, stir in the prune and Armagnac purée, then fold in the chilled whipped cream.

Now pour the mixture into the ice-cream maker and freeze-churn according to the manufacturer's instructions (you may have to do this in two batches and it will take between 30–60 minutes depending on the capacity of your machine). When the ice cream is soft-set, add the diced prune and churn it until all is incorporated then transfer to a plastic box and freeze for 2 hours before you serve. If the ice cream is made well in advance and has frozen solid, remove from the freezer for 30 minutes before serving to soften.

NOTE If you don't have an ice cream maker see page 227.

MINCE PIE ICE CREAM
SERVES 6

Sounds unlikely, doesn't it? My friend, chef Neil Nugent gave me the recipe and it really is a revelation. So easy and it's interesting when people eat it and say, 'Yes, it does taste like mince pies!'

4 shop-bought quality mince pies (or home-made if you have plenty)
300ml double cream
500g Ambrosia Devon Custard (tetra pac), refrigerated until cold

A food processor and an ice-cream maker (pre-frozen according to the manufacturer's instructions) or an electric whisk.

Preheat the oven to 140°C/gas mark 1.

Firstly, in a medium-sized bowl whip the double cream until it reaches the floppy stage but isn't too thick. Pop it into the fridge to chill.

Place the mince pies on a baking tray and put them in the oven for 10 minutes to freshen then leave them to go completely cold. Now chop the cooled mince pies fairly finely by hand (it's not really worth putting them in a food processor) then in a medium-sized bowl mix them with the cold custard before folding in the whipped cream.

Now pour the mixture into the ice-cream maker and freeze-churn according to the manufacturer's instructions (you may have to do this in two batches and it will take between 30 minutes and an hour depending on the capacity of your machine). When the ice cream is soft-set, transfer it to a plastic box and freeze for 2 hours before you serve. If the ice cream is made well in advance and has frozen solid, remove from the freezer for 30 minutes before serving to soften.

NOTE If you don't have an ice cream maker see page opposite.

CHESTNUT ICE CREAM
SERVES 4

This is another very speedy and oh so easy ice cream. No custard needed, just a glorious tin of thick chestnut pureé. You don't need to add the marrons glacés, but it does give an extra edge.

2 x 250g tins crème de marrons
    (sweetened chestnut purée)
300ml double cream
4 marrons glacés, chopped into 5mm
    cubes

An ice-cream maker (pre-frozen
    according to the manufacturer's
    instructions) or an electric whisk.

First whip the double cream until it reaches the floppy stage but isn't too thick, then stir in the crème de marrons till evenly blended.

Now pour the mixture into the ice-cream maker and freeze-churn according to the manufacturer's instructions. When the ice cream is soft-set, which may be as quick as 15 minutes, add the chopped marrons glacés and churn until it is all incorporated then transfer it to a plastic box and freeze for 2 hours before you serve. If the ice cream is made well in advance and has frozen solid, remove from the freezer for 30 minutes before serving to soften.

NOTE If you don't have an ice cream maker you can still make ice cream. After you have made up your mixture, transfer it to a lidded plastic box and put it in the coldest part of the freezer for two hours or until the contents become firm at the edges. At this stage, empty out the box into a mixing bowl and whisk the ice cream with an electric hand whisk to break down the ice crystals. Return to the plastic box and freeze for another two hours, then repeat the whisking process. Refreeze the ice cream until 30 minutes before you want to serve it.

STEM GINGER ICE CREAM
SERVES 4

What a star this is. You get the smooth velvet ice cream with the chunks of preserved ginger, which doesn't seem to freeze at all, retaining its fieriness.

6 pieces stem ginger, chopped into 5mm cubes
4 tablespoons stem ginger syrup
275ml double cream
275ml single cream
4 egg yolks
1 dessertspoon cornflour
110g golden caster sugar
1 dessertspoon ground ginger

An ice-cream maker (pre-frozen according to the manufacturer's instructions) or an electric whisk.

First whip the double cream until it reaches the floppy stage but isn't too thick, then pop it into the fridge to chill.

Next you need to make a custard, so first pour the single cream into a medium-sized saucepan, then carefully heat it to just below boiling point. Meanwhile, beat together the egg yolks, cornflour and caster sugar in a bowl until absolutely smooth. Next pour the hot cream onto this mixture, whisking as you pour. Now return the custard to the pan and continue to whisk over a medium heat until it has thickened and come to just below boiling point again (don't worry, it won't curdle – if it does look at all grainy, it will become smooth again when whisked off the heat).

Now rinse out the bowl and pour the custard into it and stir in the stem ginger syrup and the ground ginger. Then place in another larger bowl of cold water with a few ice cubes, stirring now and then until it is absolutely cold.

When the custard is completely cold, fold in the chilled whipped cream.

Now pour the mixture into the ice-cream maker and freeze-churn according to the manufacturer's instructions. When the ice cream is soft-set add the chopped ginger and churn until it is all incorporated then transfer to a plastic box and freeze for 2 hours before you serve. If the ice cream is made well in advance and has frozen solid, remove from the freezer for 30 minutes before serving to soften.

This is nice on its own but can be sprinkled with some chopped stem ginger and more syrup if you like.

NOTE If you don't have an ice cream maker see page 227.

LAST-MINUTE
Christmas

YES, I KNOW I have been plugging away at how good home-made is at Christmas. But if you find yourself with little time available, there really is no need to miss out. I have written an entire book for people who are short of time, and I know that a few minor miracles can be achieved with a little imagination. So if you are up against the clock, relax. You can still prepare a Christmas feast put together at the last minute. Read on.

PARMESAN TWISTS WITH ANCHOVY OR SESAME & POPPY SEEDS
MAKES 24

These are a doddle to make, they can be served plain with Parmesan, as in the picture, or with seeds, chopped anchovy or a mixture of them all. Just perfect for serving with drinks.

250g butter puff pastry, either rolled or
    leftover trimmings
2 tablespoons freshly grated Parmesan
2 anchovy fillets, very finely chopped
1 tablespoon sesame seeds
1 tablespoon poppy seeds
1 small egg, beaten
flour (for rolling)
seasoning

Two large baking sheets, lightly
    greased.

Begin by rolling out the pastry on a lightly floured surface to an oblong roughly 30 x 23cm, then divide it into 2 pieces (15 x 23cm).

Then take one of the pieces of pastry and brush it well with beaten egg. After that sprinkle the Parmesan evenly all over, followed by the pieces of anchovy, and press it all down into the pastry either with your fingers or a palette knife. Now brush the second piece of pastry with beaten egg and sprinkle it evenly with a mixture of the sesame and poppy seeds and again press the seeds well into the pastry and add some seasoning.

Now place both the pastry sheets on a lightly floured tray and chill them for about 30 minutes, so they are easier to cut and twist. Then cut each piece into 12 evenly sized long strips and place each one on the baking tray. Now, holding down one end, twist them round and round, before pressing the other end on to the baking tray. (You can now cover and chill the twists if you don't want to cook them straight away.)

When you're ready to cook them preheat the oven to 200°C/gas mark 6, pop them in the oven and bake for 12–14 minutes, until they are puffed and golden brown. They can be made ahead and warmed through in the oven. Alternatively, once cooked, you can freeze them till needed – in which case put them on a baking sheet and pop them in the oven at the same temperature for 5 minutes.

TURKEY ROULADES WITH PORK, SAGE & ONION STUFFING

SERVES 4

My friend Liz always makes this at Christmas because she can't, she says, do the whole turkey thing. It's no trouble to prepare, easy to serve and you still get all the lovely flavours of a traditional Christmas lunch.

FOR THE TURKEY

4 turkey breast escalopes or steaks,
    approximately 175g each
400g smoked streaky bacon,
    derinded (16 rashers)

FOR THE STUFFING

350g pork sausagemeat
10g chopped sage
1 small onion, very finely chopped
25g fresh white breadcrumbs
freshly milled black pepper

FOR THE GRAVY

1 rounded dessertspoon plain flour
200ml dry white wine
200ml chicken stock
seasoning

A medium roasting tin, lightly greased.

First of all, take the turkey escalopes and place them one at a time between two pieces of clingfilm. Take a rolling pin and gently roll each escalope so it measures about 23cm long by 10cm wide and 5mm thick (it doesn't matter if these measurements are not perfect!). If you are using steaks they will need to be battened out with the rolling pin.

Next mix the stuffing ingredients together. Then take a quarter of the stuffing and roll it into a sausage the same length as the escalope (dampen your hands with water if the stuffing is sticky) and place the sausage-shaped stuffing 2.5cm from one side of the length of an escalope and carefully roll the turkey around the stuffing. Repeat with the other escalopes. Then, taking one rasher of bacon, wrap it round one of the roulades, starting at one end, overlapping it slightly, then carry on with three more slices until the roulade is completely wrapped. Repeat with the other 3 roulades. Cover and chill for a minimum of 2 hours.

When you are ready to cook the turkey, preheat the oven to 200°C/ gas mark 6. Place the 4 roulades, well apart, in the greased roasting tin and roast on the middle shelf of the oven for 50–55 minutes, or until crispy and firm to the touch. Remove the roulades from the tin and then cover them with a sheet of foil to keep warm.

To make the gravy, place the roasting tin over direct heat turned to fairly low, sprinkle in the plain flour and whisk until smooth. Then mix the wine with the stock and add it, little by little. Whisk thoroughly until the stock and wine are incorporated, and bring it to simmering point, then let it bubble and reduce for about 5 minutes. Then taste and season if necessary and pour into a warmed serving jug.

To serve, slice each roulade diagonally into 3 or 4 pieces and place on a warm serving dish.

CRISP GRESSINGHAM DUCK BREASTS WITH A PORT & BITTER ORANGE SAUCE
SERVES 6

In spite of the length of the instructions this really is very easy to prepare and, because the duck is reheated, it's all done in advance, so you will have more time at the table.

6 Gressingham duck breast fillets,
    about 200g each
seasoning
watercress, to garnish
FOR THE SAUCE
1 medium orange
1 dessertspoon plain flour
150ml stock (made with Marigold
    bouillon)
1 dessertspoon lemon juice
75ml port
1 rounded teaspoon dark brown sugar

Two large frying pans and a grill pan
    with a rack.

To prepare the duck, put both frying pans on a medium to low heat then, using a fork, prick the skin of each duck breast and, with a small, sharp knife, score the skin diagonally both ways to form a diamond pattern and season. Now pop three fillets into each pan, skin-side down, and cook very gently for 20 minutes until most of the fat has rendered and the skin is a light golden brown. The fat will bubble gently around the edge of the duck but don't let it get too hot or the skin will colour too quickly.

After that carefully drain off the duck fat (you can keep it for roasting potatoes and you will need some for the sauce), then turn each breast over and (without increasing the heat) cook them for 5 minutes if you like it pink, 10 for medium and 15 for well done. Now transfer them to a plate (keeping the skin side up) and leave them on one side in a cool place until you are ready to reheat them.

Now make the sauce. Pare off just the outer zest of the orange – a potato peeler is useful here. Then using a sharp knife, cut the zest into very thin shreds (you can layer up the pieces of zest a few at a time to do this). Blanch the shreds in some boiling water for 2–3 minutes then drain them and keep on one side, and squeeze the orange.

Next heat 1 tablespoon of the rendered duck fat in a small saucepan over a medium heat and use a wooden spoon to stir in the flour and when it is smooth cook for a minute. Now switch to a whisk and begin to add in the stock, whisking all the time as you add it. Add the orange and lemon juice, the blanched orange zest, the sugar and some seasoning, then let it cook for a few minutes. Just before serving add the port and transfer to a warm serving jug.

About 20 minutes before you want to serve the duck, preheat the grill to its highest setting, making sure the grill pan will be about 11cm from the heat source. When the grill has been heating for at least 10 minutes, place the duck breasts skin-side down on the rack of the grill pan and place them under the grill for 2–3 minutes until they are hot. Then turn them over and grill them for a further 2 minutes – keep an eye on them as the skin will sizzle and crisp as it turns a deeper golden brown.

Remove them to a carving board to rest for a few minutes before slicing them into thick chunky slices onto warm plates. Drizzle some sauce over and garnish with watercress.

POT-ROASTED TURKEY DRUMSTICKS WITH PORT, BACON & CHESTNUTS
SERVES 6

Over recent years turkey crowns have become very popular – but the actual price was about the same as a whole bird. However, the rather neglected drumsticks have a wonderful richness and succulence, and are available at much lower cost. Other good news too – this recipe can be made ahead and reheated.

2 turkey drumsticks, each weighing about 700g

1 tablespoon butter

1 tablespoon groundnut oil

12 rashers smoked streaky bacon, each one rolled up tightly and secured with a cocktail stick

18 shallots, peeled

2 cloves garlic, peeled and chopped

300ml red wine

50ml port

250ml stock (made with Marigold bouillon)

2 bay leaves

6 sprigs thyme

200g frozen peeled chestnuts, defrosted (or vac-packed)

1 heaped tablespoon plain flour mixed with 1 heaped tablespoon soft butter

seasoning

FOR THE STUFFING

450g sausagemeat

20g chopped sage

1 medium onion, very finely chopped

40g fresh white breadcrumbs

1 dessertspoon plain flour

A large heavy-based, lidded 3.5 litre casserole.

First prepare the stuffing by mixing the sausagemeat, onion, sage and breadcrumbs with some seasoning and divide it into 12 even-sized pieces. Then with floured hands, shape the stuffing pieces into balls using the palms of your hands.

Next melt half the butter and oil in the casserole and while that's happening, wipe the turkey drumsticks as dry as possible with kitchen paper and season them. When the butter begins to sizzle, place the drumsticks in the hot fat then, with the heat at medium, brown them on all sides, using a spoon and fork to turn them around until they are a nice golden colour (which will take about 10 minutes). After that remove the turkey drumsticks to a large plate.

Next brown the bacon rolls, followed by the shallots, and as they brown take them out to join the turkey drumsticks, removing the cocktail sticks from the bacon. Now add the rest of the butter and oil and, when it's hot, brown the stuffing balls turning them frequently until golden, which will take about 15 minutes, remove them. Finally add the garlic to the pan, which will need about 1 minute, tossing it around to colour it. Then return the turkey to the casserole and add the wine, port, stock, bay leaves and thyme. Bring it up to a gentle simmer, turn the heat down, put the lid on and cook for 30 minutes.

After that add the chestnuts straight from the freezer, along with the shallots. Bring it all back to simmering point, then with the lid on give it 60 minutes, adding the stuffing balls and bacon rolls for the last 15 minutes. When it's cooked, transfer the drumsticks and all the other ingredients to a plate, using a draining spoon, and discard the bay leaves and thyme. Then add the butter-and-flour in small ½ teaspoon-sized lumps to the sauce in the casserole, and whisk the sauce back up to simmering point to thicken it.

When the turkey is cool enough to handle, pull away and discard all the skin, then carefully ease the meat away from the bone, keeping it in quite large, chunky pieces. Discard any of the fine bones and pieces of cartilage, then return the meat and other ingredients to the sauce.

If you're preparing ahead, decant into a container when it is completely cold, cover and chill till needed. Back in the casserole, it will take 30–40 minutes' gentle simmering to reheat.

LAST-MINUTE BRANDIED CHRISTMAS CAKE

Yes, I know, it's happened to me too. You meant to make a Christmas cake in early October, feed it weekly with brandy, let it mature, marzipan it two weeks before and ice it a week before the big day – and guess what, you didn't! All is not lost, though. There is a very simple home-made version to hand for those who didn't get round to it, or are fearful of making one for the first time, and it's also extremely good. It's made with a jar of luxury mincemeat, which gives it a beautifully moist texture, and topped with whole nuts, which get nicely toasted during the baking (a great topping for those who don't like it too sweet). However, should you wish, it would be easy to put ready-made marzipan and fondant icing (see page 32) on instead of the nuts.

FOR THE PRE-SOAKING

150ml brandy

1 x 400g (approximately) jar luxury
   mincemeat

110g no-soak prunes, roughly chopped

50g glacé cherries, quartered

175g dried mixed fruit

50g whole candied peel, finely chopped

FOR THE CAKE

225g self-raising flour, sifted

3 teaspoons baking powder

150g softened butter

150g dark muscovado sugar

the grated zest of 1 small orange

the grated zest of 1 small lemon

50g Brazil nuts, roughly chopped

50g mixed chopped nuts

3 eggs

1½ teaspoons mixed spice

FOR THE TOPPING

approximately 18 walnut halves,
   18 pecan halves, 20 whole Brazils
   (or any other mixture you like)

1 heaped tablespoon sieved apricot jam

1 tablespoon brandy

A 20cm round cake tin, lightly oiled,
   the base and sides lined with
   baking parchment.

Begin the cake a few hours before you want to make it (or even the night before) and simply place all the pre-soaking ingredients into a bowl, stir really well, then cover with a cloth and leave in a cool place.

When you are ready to make the cake, preheat the oven to 170°C/ gas mark 3. Take a roomy bowl and simply place the soaked ingredients plus all the rest of the cake ingredients in it, all in one go (it's helpful to tick them off as they go in). Now, preferably using an electric hand whisk (or a wooden spoon), beat everything together as thoroughly as possible, which will probably take about 1 minute. Then pour it into the prepared tin, level the top and arrange the whole nuts either in rows or in circles on the surface.

Finally, cover the top of the cake with a double square of baking parchment with a hole the size of a 50p piece cut in the centre. Then place the cake on the centre shelf of the oven and bake it for about 1½–2 hours or until the centre springs back when lightly touched. Then let it cool in the tin for 30 minutes before turning it out to finish cooling on a wire rack, removing the lining papers.

The finishing touch is to heat the apricot jam and brandy together and brush the nuts with the mixture to give them a lovely glaze. Store the cake in an airtight tin or in double baking parchment and foil and it will keep beautifully moist for 3 to 4 weeks. For a festive touch you might like to tie a ribbon and bow all round for the big day.

MINI CHRISTMAS PUDDINGS
SERVES 4

These are made in moments and, like the previous cake, are made with mincemeat and cooked in less than an hour, are light-textured but have all the flavours of Christmas. You don't have to make them at the last minute – they freeze beautifully and reheat like a dream. Serve with Christmas Rum Sauce (see page 266) or Cumberland Rum Butter (see page 78).

200g mincemeat
60g self-raising flour
½ teaspoon baking powder
½ rounded teaspoon ground mixed spice
1 medium egg
25g softened butter
40ml black treacle
55ml Irish stout
1 tablespoon dark rum
40g Bramley apple, peeled, cored and finely diced
10g roasted chopped hazelnuts
75g currants
the grated zest of ½ orange
the grated zest of ½ lemon
1 tablespoon brandy, if flaming the puddings

Four 175ml mini non-stick pudding basins, well buttered, a small shallow roasting tin, some baking parchment and foil.

Preheat the oven to 180°C/gas mark 4.

First sift the flour, baking powder and mixed spice into a medium mixing bowl, then add the egg and softened butter. After that, measure the treacle into a glass measuring jug, add the stout and rum and mix these together. Next pour this mixture into the bowl and, using an electric hand whisk, whisk everything very thoroughly together.

Now add the apple, nuts, currants, mincemeat and, finally, the grated orange and lemon zests. Then mix everything together very thoroughly, and divide the mixture among the 4 well-buttered pudding basins. Top each with a small circle of buttered baking parchment, followed by an 18cm square of foil large enough to fold under the edges of the basins, making a pleat all the way round to seal. Now place the basins in the tin and pour in 2.5cm of boiling water from the kettle, then place the tin in the oven and leave to cook for 45–50 minutes, or until the puddings are springy and firm to the touch in the centre. Then remove them from the oven, remove the foil and baking parchment and let them stand for 10 minutes before carefully running a small knife around each one to turn them out on to warm serving plates.

If you want to flame the puddings, this is very easy to do and it's guaranteed to impress your guests. Firstly line the puddings up on a warm serving platter, then warm the brandy in a metal ladle over direct heat and, as soon as the brandy is hot, turn out the flame and ask someone to set light to it using a long match. Place the ladle now gently flaming over one of the puddings – but don't pour the brandy over until you reach the table. (If you don't have a gas hob, warm the brandy in a small saucepan.) When you do, pour it slowly over all the puddings and watch them flame to the cheers of the assembled company.

NOTE The photograph includes cranberries which look festive but are not really needed.

CARIBBEAN BANANA & RAISIN STRUDEL
SERVES 6

Whilst sometimes *feuilles de brick* (brick pastry – see page 59) has the edge on filo, for strudel nothing can compare with its lovely buttery, crunchy layers. This one made with bananas and rum has a very Christmassy feel. Serve it with large dollops of crème fraîche.

4 medium bananas
50g raisins
the grated zest of 1 large navel orange
2 tablespoons rum
100g pecan nuts
75g butter
4 sheets filo pastry, about 24 x 50cm, defrosted
2 heaped tablespoons crème fraîche
1 tablespoon icing sugar, for sprinkling

A large baking sheet, lightly greased.

Ideally a couple of hours before you start, soak the raisins and orange zest in the rum. After that, drain the raisins and zest in a sieve over a bowl to catch the juices, pressing to extract as much juice as possible.

When you're ready to start preheat the oven to 180°C/gas mark 4 and pop the nuts on the baking tray to toast for 5–6 minutes and at the same time melt the butter in a saucepan. Then remove the nuts and pulse them in a processor to chop them small. Now spread out a sheet of baking parchment on the tray. Follow this with one sheet of filo pastry (cover the others with a clean tea towel). Brush the filo pastry all over with melted butter and sprinkle on a quarter of the nuts.

Do this another three times with the rest of the filo pastry (saving some butter for the top). Now peel the bananas and lay two, end to end, about 5cm from one edge of the pastry. Place the other two bananas directly next to them towards the middle. Next scatter the raisins and zest over the bananas.

The strained rum juice now needs to be whisked into the crème fraîche, then spoon this over the bananas. Use the baking parchment to help you roll the filo pastry over the bananas and then over again. Trim 2.5cm off each end of the filo parcel, then tuck the ends under – so you are left with the seam and the ends underneath – and discard the parchment. Brush the rest of the butter all over and bake on the centre shelf for 40 minutes. If you like you can make the strudel a few hours in advance and bake it when you want to serve it. Sprinkle with icing sugar before serving.

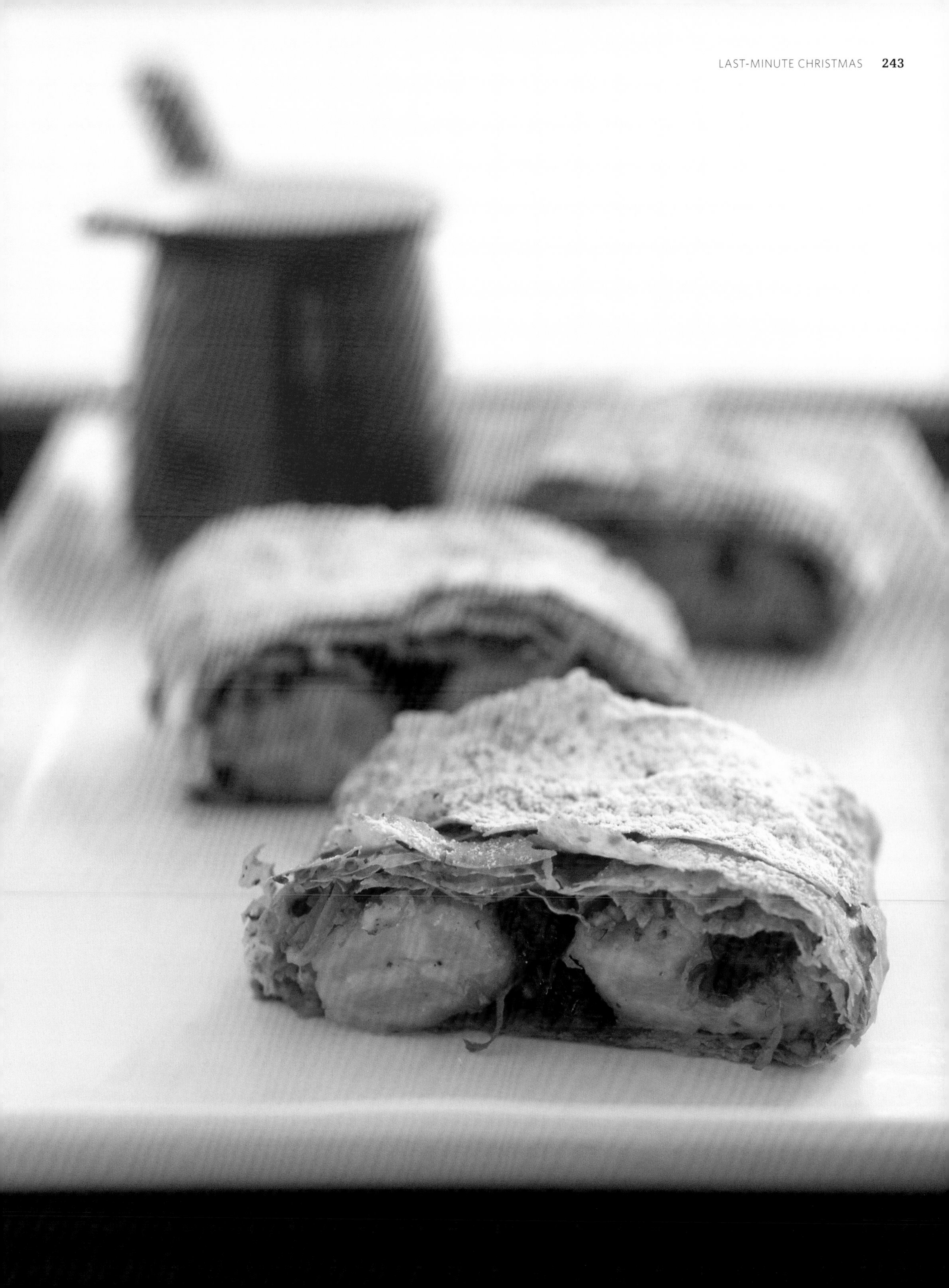

VANILLA BEAN ICE CREAM WITH RAISINS SOAKED IN PEDRO XIMÉNEZ SHERRY

SERVES 4

Pedro Ximénez sherry is sweet, nutty and tastes of raisins. An easy instant dessert with a wonderful combination of flavours. If you have some good-quality vanilla bean ice cream stashed away in the freezer, the raisins will keep in a jar as long as you want, and you can serve it any time you like.

good-quality vanilla bean ice cream
100g muscatel (or any large) raisins
4 tablespoons Pedro Ximénez sherry

Put the raisins and sherry in a screw-top jar, give it a shake and store in a cool place for at least a week. Serve scoops of ice cream topped with raisins and sherry – and give everyone a glass of Pedro Ximénez on the side.

A TRIFLE EASIER
SERVES 4-6

The ingredients here might raise a few eyebrows, but the proof of the pudding is still in the eating and I promise you'll want to keep eating this! I find that there are those who like jelly trifles and those who prefer custard and cream only. So, if you are one of the latter, cut out the jelly bit, pour the custard over the sponge and top with 275ml whipped cream before adding the nuts. With the jelly version below, no whipped cream but some chilled pouring cream over each portion at the table would be brilliant.

5 trifle sponges
3 heaped tablespoons Seville orange marmalade
150ml Madeira (or dry sherry)
1 x 410g tin orange segments (or mandarin oranges)
2 medium bananas
7g leaf gelatine (4 sheets measuring about 11 x 7.5cm each)
570ml freshly squeezed orange juice
FOR THE TOPPING
500g Ambrosia Devon Custard (tetra pac)
1 teaspoon pure vanilla extract
355ml double cream
30g toasted flaked almonds

A 1.75 litre glass bowl.

First of all, split the trifle sponges in half lengthways, then spread one half of each sponge with marmalade and form them back into sandwiches. Cut each one across into three and arrange the pieces, cut side uppermost, in the base of a glass bowl. Stab each one with a sharp knife, then carefully pour the Madeira all over the sponges and leave them to soak for about 30 minutes (tilting the bowl a couple of times to encourage this).

Meanwhile, drain the oranges, pressing them to squeeze out the juice, then arrange them over the sponges. Now peel and slice the bananas into chunks about 5mm thick and scatter these in among the oranges.

For the jelly: snip the gelatine leaves with scissors into strips into a small saucepan and cover them with 150ml of orange juice. Leave to soak for 5 minutes then place the pan over a medium heat and whisk for a minute until the gelatine has dissolved. Now whisk this into the rest of the juice and pour it over the contents of the bowl. Leave to set, covered in the fridge.

Finally, place the cream and vanilla in a medium-sized bowl and whip it to the floppy stage – be careful not to make it too thick. After that fold in the custard till evenly blended. Pour the whole lot over the trifle and spread it out evenly. Cover with clingfilm and chill again in the fridge, sprinkling with the toasted almonds before serving.

CARAMELISED TOFFEE PECAN TARTS WITH CLOTTED CREAM
SERVES 4

I can't believe this one is so easy and at the same time will provide a very elegant sweet dish to end a meal. Making your own tartlet cases is a real fiddle, but I have to say the ready-made butter cases are brilliant.

4 all-butter tartlet cases
5 rounded tablespoons rich caramel
    toffee sauce (about 250ml)
150g pecans
chilled clotted cream, to serve

A small baking tray.

Preheat the grill to its highest setting
    for a minimum of 10 minutes.

First warm the toffee sauce in a small pan or in a microwave bowl.

Place the tartlet cases on a baking tray, then in another bowl combine the pecans with two-thirds of the warmed sauce, tossing them all around to get a good coating. Now spoon these into the tartlet cases and top each one with the rest of the sauce.

Now place the tray under the grill 10cm from the heat and watch carefully. Wait until the tarts warm up and the sauce begins to bubble and caramelise (about 1–2 minutes). Serve warm from the grill with clotted cream. (You can assemble these in advance and just grill before serving.)

BANANAS BAKED IN RUM WITH RUM SYLLABUB
SERVES 6

The ease and simplicity of this recipe belie its excellent depth and flavour – definitely one of those recipes that tastes infinitely better than it sounds. Serve it straight from the oven with the chilled syllabub, or it tastes every bit as good cold.

6 bananas, cut into 4cm slices on the diagonal
75g large raisins
3 tablespoons dark rum
3 tablespoons molasses sugar
1 dessertspoon freshly grated orange zest (with a zester)
1 teaspoon freshly grated lime zest (with a zester)
2 tablespoons freshly squeezed orange juice
1 tablespoon freshly squeezed lime juice

FOR THE SYLLABUB
2 tablespoons dark rum
2 tablespoons lime juice
1 tablespoon molasses sugar
150ml double cream
whole nutmeg, for grating

A shallow 20 x 28cm gratin dish, buttered.

You need to start this off about half an hour before you intend to cook the bananas by placing the raisins in a small basin, along with the rum, then leave them aside to soak for abou 30 minutes to plump up.

Next, make the syllabub. Measure the rum and lime juice into a medium-sized bowl, add the sugar, give it a whisk and leave for 10 minutes to allow the sugar to dissolve. Then pour in the cream and, using an electric hand whisk, beat until it stands in soft peaks and cover with clingfilm and chill until needed.

When you're ready to cook the bananas, preheat the oven to 180°C/ gas mark 4. Then sprinkle half the molasses sugar over the base of the gratin dish and arrange the bananas on top. Now sprinkle the rum and raisins over them, followed by the orange and lime zest and juice, and finally the remaining sugar.

Now cover the dish with foil and then place it on the top shelf of the oven and cook the bananas for about 20–25 minutes. After that, remove the foil and then give them a further 5 minutes.

Just before serving, re-whisk the syllabub and spoon over the bananas and lastly, grate a little nutmeg on top.

LITTLE MINCEMEAT SOUFFLÉ PUDDINGS
with Chilled Rum Sabayon
SERVES 8

These little soufflé-like puddings are what I would call very well behaved! You can cook them in advance and reheat them, and they will rise up again. You can even freeze them – if you want to make these puddings ahead, they will reheat at the same temperature in 15 minutes (or 20 from frozen). You can serve them in the dishes or I quite like them turned out.

110g mincemeat
110g butter, at room temperature
110g caster sugar
6 eggs, separated
175g light ginger cake, reduced to fine
    crumbs in a food processor
a generous pinch of ground cloves
¼ teaspoon ground cinnamon
the grated zest of ½ lemon
a little icing sugar

Eight ramekin dishes with a base
    measurement of 7.5cm,
    well buttered, and a shallow
    roasting tin.

Preheat the oven to 180°C/gas mark 4.

First, arrange the ramekins in a shallow roasting tin. Next, in a mixing bowl, cream the butter and half of the sugar together until the mixture is pale and fluffy. Then beat in the egg yolks a little at a time. Fold in the cake crumbs, followed by the spices, mincemeat and lemon zest. Now put the kettle on to boil.

Now, in a separate bowl, whisk the egg whites until they stand in soft peaks and gradually whisk in the remaining sugar. What you will now have is a meringue mixture. Take one heaped tablespoonful and fold it in to loosen the mincemeat mixture, then the rest should be carefully folded in. Spoon an equal quantity of the mixture into each ramekin, then pour approximately 1cm of boiling water into the roasting tin and transfer it to the centre of the oven to bake for 25 minutes.

Turn the puddings out on to warm serving plates by sliding a palette knife round the edges, then tipping each one out upside down. You can flip them right side up if you prefer. Dust with a little sifted icing sugar and serve the Chilled Rum Sabayon separately.

CHILLED RUM SABAYON

2–3 tablespoons rum
4 egg yolks
50g caster sugar
4 tablespoons freshly squeezed orange juice

Begin by placing a heatproof bowl over a saucepan of barely simmering water (don't let the bowl sit in the water). Then add the egg yolks and the sugar, and whisk together until frothy. Next add the orange juice and rum, and continue to whisk vigorously with an electric whisk for about 8 minutes, until the sauce is thick and foamy. Be careful not to let the water under the bowl rise above a bare simmer during this time. Sorry, I have tried every which way to get the right result without standing by for 8 minutes, but failed – however it is worth it. Remove the bowl from the heat. Cool, cover and chill thoroughly in the fridge. Taste before serving and, if you like, add some extra rum!

The
LAST 36 HOURS

I HAVE RETAINED THIS chapter more or less as it was, simply because so many people have found it helpful (including me, it has to be said). It's a kind of chronology of all that the cook needs to do in the final 36 hours leading up to Christmas lunch. Even if you're not serving the traditional lunch set out below, you may still find it helpful to see some sort of framework into which different recipes can be inserted.

Don't forget, too, that sometimes people drop in unexpectedly at Christmas. That's one of the lovely things about it, and you just have to accept that you might be taking off your apron and pouring drinks just when you thought you had space to make the mince pies! So, given the inevitable disruptions, this countdown is not a rigid, must-be-obeyed sort of thing, but rather a few gentle reminders to help you through some busy hours.

Christmas Eve

early am

LAST-MINUTE SHOPPING

In practice this means sallying forth for the freshest vegetables (sprouts, leeks, parsnips, onions, carrots, celery, swede, potatoes) and fruit (oranges, clementines, grapes, bananas, dates, cranberries), because they need to last over the whole holiday. Everyone else will be doing the same, of course, so do get out early and, before you leave the house, read the various shopping lists (see pages 22–23) *out loud*. You may have forgotten something. Have you got milk, cream, bread, pet food, the turkey . . .?

mid-morning

THE TURKEY ARRIVES

Now at last your fresh and magnificent bird has reached its destination. There is no need to wash or wipe it, just place it on a sheet of greaseproof paper and remove the giblets. Make sure you know what it weighs: your supplier should have written it down – if not, you might find the bathroom scales helpful, but make sure you keep it on the greaseproof paper. Store it (uncovered) in the fridge till just before you go to bed. You may well need to remove one shelf from the fridge to house it, but if space is a desperate problem, don't worry: you can use an unheated bedroom, or the garage (with suitable covering) – even, in an emergency, the locked boot of the car, which can be pretty cold on a winter's night.

GIBLET STOCK

However unpromising the giblets look, they make a wonderful stock for the turkey gravy.

the turkey giblets, including the neck and, if you're not
   using it for stuffing (see page 256), the liver
1 onion, sliced in half
1 carrot, sliced in half lengthways
a few parsley stalks
1 celery stalk, plus a few leaves
1 bay leaf
6 whole black peppercorns
salt
900ml water

First wash the giblets and put them in a saucepan with the halved onion, then cover with the water and bring up to simmering point. After removing any surface scum with a draining spoon, add the remaining ingredients, half-cover the pan with a lid and simmer for 1½–2 hours. Then strain the stock, cool and store, covered, in the fridge. I always think that it's when the giblet stock is simmering that you get the first fragrant aromas of Christmas lunch, which fill you with the pleasure of anticipation!

later am

PREPARING VEGETABLES

A good time to get these chores out of the way. Always my choice for Christmas lunch are the tiny, tight button sprouts and I prefer to serve them plain as there are so many other rich flavours around. Prepare 700g–1 kg for 8–10 people, and keep them stored in a polythene bag in the fridge till needed. Another regular is parsnips: my recipe for these is Parsnips with Parmesan (see page 193). They can be prepared in advance right up to the oven-ready stage. Store them laid out on a tray in the fridge or a cool place. Also at this stage, if you're serving them with drinks, take the sausage rolls out of the freezer to defrost for an hour, then warm them in the oven for 5 minutes.

early pm

MAKE THE TRIFLE

Christmas simply isn't Christmas without a trifle. I find this is the best time to assemble it.

3 pm

CAROLS & BAKING

It used to be a tradition in our house to see to all the Christmas baking to the backdrop of the live broadcast of the *Festival of Nine Lessons and Carols* from King's College, Cambridge. But now I just take them ready-cooked from the freezer as and when I need them, and enjoy eating the warmed mince pies with my feet up and a cup of tea listening to the carols. This is the moment when Christmas really begins for me. (To warm the mince pies from frozen they should have 45 minutes out of the freezer to defrost, then be placed in a medium oven for 5 minutes and dusted with icing sugar before serving.)

later pm

THE TURKEY STUFFING

Now is the time to make up the stuffing ready to go into the turkey tomorrow. I firmly believe that the whole idea of stuffing a large bird like a turkey is to help to counteract the drying-out process during cooking. Minced pork (or pork sausagemeat) is an ideal ingredient for this because the fatty juices from the pork help to keep the flesh of the turkey moist. For this reason all the stuffings below have pork as a main ingredient. All the stuffings are for a 5.5–6.5kg turkey.

NOTE If you like your stuffing firm, so that it cuts in slices, add a beaten egg to bind it. If, like me, you prefer it crumbly, leave the egg out. Also, it is important to remember to remove the stuffing from the fridge before you go to bed and leave it covered in a cool place – it shouldn't be too chilled when it goes into the turkey.

EIGHTEENTH-CENTURY CHESTNUT STUFFING

This recipe is adapted from one I first came across in the cookery book written by the eighteenth-century writer, Hannah Glasse. Peeling chestnuts is a chore at the best of times, but with the pressures of Christmas it can seem even more tiresome. So, if you can get hold of very good frozen peeled or vacuum-packed chestnuts these will make life infinitely easier.

450g frozen peeled chestnuts,
    defrosted (or vac-packed)
1 large onion, finely chopped
110g smoked streaky bacon,
    finely chopped
the liver from the turkey, chopped small
25g butter
225g best-quality pork sausagemeat or
    finely minced pure pork
4 tablespoons chopped parsley
1 dessertspoon chopped thyme
¼ teaspoon ground mace
seasoning

Melt the butter in a large frying-pan and cook the onion, bacon and chopped turkey liver for 10 minutes or so, until the onion looks transparent and everything is tinged gold at the edges. Now tip the contents of the pan into a large mixing bowl and add all the remaining ingredients. Season and mix very thoroughly.

AMERICAN TURKEY STUFFING

This type of stuffing was first served to me at a delightful Thanksgiving Dinner given by some American friends. The recipe, as many are, was handed down from grandmother to mother to daughter. This is my own adaptation, which keeps the variety of flavours and textures.

175g white bread, cut into 1cm cubes
225g onions, chopped fairly small
4 sticks celery, cut into 1cm chunks
450g best-quality thin pork sausages, skinned and sliced into 1cm chunks
225g Bramley apples, cored and chopped (no need to peel)
110g walnuts, chopped
50g butter
1 dessertspoon chopped thyme
the grated zest of 1 small lemon
½ teaspoon ground mace
seasoning

Begin by melting the butter in a large frying-pan and lightly fry the chopped onions, celery and chunks of sausage until they become golden at the edges (this will take about 10 minutes). After that tip these into a large mixing bowl and add all the remaining ingredients. Mix very thoroughly, seasoning well.

TRADITIONAL PORK, SAGE & ONION STUFFING

This might seem like a large amount, but we love it cold with leftover turkey or in sandwiches. If you prefer not to, make half the amount.

900g good-quality pork sausagemeat
  or finely minced pure pork
25g sage, chopped
75g stale white bread, crusts removed
1 large onion, cut into chunks
2 tablespoons water
seasoning

In a processor add the bread in chunks with the motor running until you have breadcrumbs, then add the sage leaves and chunks of onion and process these till finely chopped. Now, in a bowl, combine the sausagemeat with the breadcrumb mixture and the water very thoroughly using a large fork or your hands. Add some seasoning, then place the stuffing in a large polythene bag, and store in the fridge until needed.

early evening

ACCOMPANIMENTS

In our family there are those who like bread sauce as the accompaniment to turkey and there are those who prefer cranberries – and there are some of us who have both! The following is quite positively the best cranberry sauce I've ever tasted *and* it's oh, so easy to make.

CRANBERRY & ORANGE RELISH
SERVES 8

450g fresh cranberries
the rind and juice of 1 large navel orange
1 heaped teaspoon freshly grated root ginger or
    ½ teaspoon ground ginger
75g caster sugar
A 4cm piece of cinnamon
4 cloves
2–3 tablespoons port

Chop the cranberries in a food processor, then place them in a saucepan. Now pare off the zest of the orange with a potato peeler and cut it into very fine shreds. Add these, with the juice of the orange, to the pan, followed by the ginger, sugar and spices. Bring everything up to simmering point, stir well, put a lid on the pan and let it all simmer very gently for about 5 minutes – a timer is useful here (I often forget about it). Then remove the pan from the heat, stir in the port and, when it has cooled, pour into a serving dish. Cover with clingfilm and keep in a cool place or in the fridge till needed. Don't forget to remove the cloves and cinnamon before serving!

NOTE If you have any left over it's great served with pâté and potted meats and keeps well in the fridge for up to 2 weeks.

GET AHEAD!

If you're still on your feet by this time, you can also prepare the onion and cloves ready for the Traditional Bread Sauce (see page 266) and place in a saucepan covered with clingfilm. And why not weigh out the butter and sugar for the Christmas Rum Sauce (see page 266) and cover them in a saucepan ready for the off tomorrow?

BEFORE YOU GO TO BED

In my younger days I used to dash off to Midnight Mass and return home with a group of friends for spiced cider, sausage rolls and pickled shallots at about 1.30 am. Nowadays I like a good night's sleep before cooking the Christmas lunch, so I opt for an early night and morning Mass instead. Early or late, though, it is important to *take the turkey out of the fridge* now to allow it to come to room temperature so that it heats up immediately when you put it in the oven. The same applies to the stuffing, store them covered in a cool place, and you also need to remove 75g of butter to soften ready for the morning. Now your fridge will be looking on the empty side, so it's a good time to slip in the white wine, champagne, mineral water, children's drinks and anything else that needs to be chilled.

Christmas Day

early am

WHAT TIME IS LUNCH?

The specific timings that follow are those tested over the years in our house, but because lunch time will vary from one family to another you can adjust these timings to suit yourself. With young children you will doubtless be up early and want to eat lunch reasonably early; with older children it's not quite so important to open the presents at the first light of dawn!

For an average family-sized 6.5kg turkey (oven-ready weight) I am calculating for a 2.00 pm lunch. If you plan to eat half an hour later or earlier, simply add or subtract 30 minutes to or from my timings.

PRINCIPLES OF TURKEY COOKING

Many people have their own favourite way to cook turkey, usually because it's the way they were taught. I'm sure there is no best way, and I offer you the following method simply because it has always worked well for me and countless others. The turkey is placed in a 'tent' of foil, which essentially means it cooks in an oven within an oven. If you wrap the foil too closely to the turkey, though, it ends up steaming instead of roasting. Give it plenty of space between the flesh and the foil and it will roast in its own buttery juices without becoming dry. This method keeps all the juices intact. If you allow the bird to rest for 30–45 minutes before carving all the juices which have bubbled up to the surface will seep back and ensure the meat is moist and succulent.

COOKING TIMES FOR OTHER-SIZED TURKEYS

3.5–4.5kg turkey

30 minutes at 220°C/gas mark 7, then 2½–3 hours at 170°C/gas mark 3, and a final 30 minutes (uncovered) at 200°C/gas mark 6.

6.75–9kg turkey

45 minutes at 220°C/gas mark 7, then 4–5 hours at 170°C/gas mark 3, and a final 30 minutes (uncovered) at 200°C/gas mark 6.

Please bear in mind that ovens and turkeys themselves vary and the only one sure way to know your turkey is cooked is to pierce the thickest part of the leg with a thin skewer, the juices running out of it should be golden and clear (there should be no trace of pinkness). You can also give the leg a little tug to make sure there is some give in it.

TRADITIONAL ROAST TURKEY
FOR A 6.5KG TURKEY. SEE PAGE 263 FOR TIMINGS FOR OTHER WEIGHTS OF TURKEY.

It's only dangerous to put turkey stuffing inside the body cavity if either the turkey or the stuffing is not defrosted properly, because the heat will not penetrate it quickly enough. If both are at room temperature it is perfectly safe.

6.5kg turkey, oven-ready
75g butter, softened
225g very fat streaky bacon
seasoning
1 quantity of stuffing (see pages 256–259)

Extra-wide strong turkey foil and a small skewer or cocktail sticks.

7.45 am
Preheat the oven to 220°C/gas mark 7.

First stuff the turkey with your chosen stuffing. Loosen the skin with your hands and pack the stuffing into the neck end, pushing it up between the flesh and the skin towards the breast (not too tightly, because it will expand during the cooking). Press it in gently to make a nicely rounded end, then tuck the neck flap under the bird's back and secure with a small skewer or some cocktail sticks. Don't expect to get all the stuffing in this end – put the rest into the body cavity.

Now arrange two large sheets of foil across your roasting tin, one widthways and the other lengthways (no need to butter them). Lay the turkey on its back in the centre, then rub it generously all over with the butter, making sure the thigh bones are particularly well covered. Next season the bird all over and lay the bacon over the breast with the rashers overlapping each other. I always put some over the legs as well.

Now wrap the turkey loosely in the foil. The parcel must be firmly sealed but roomy enough to provide an air space around most of the upper part of the bird. So bring one piece of foil up and fold both ends over to make a pleat along the length of the breastbone. Then bring the other piece up at both ends and crimp and fold to make a neat parcel.

8.15 am
Place the turkey in the preheated oven, where it will cook at the initial high temperature for 40 minutes.

Once it is in, you can peel the potatoes ready for roasting and keep them covered with cold water in a saucepan.

Because of the sausagemeat stuffing and the bacon rashers already on the bird, we don't serve bacon rolls and chipolatas. But if you do, now is the time to prepare them as follows: brush a shallow baking tray with oil and arrange the sausages on it in two rows. For the bacon rolls, stretch the rinded rashers out as far as you can, then roll them up very tightly, thread them on to long flat skewers and place them next to the chipolatas and pop them all back in the fridge ready to go in the oven at 1.15 pm.

Now begin making the bread sauce.

TRADITIONAL BREAD SAUCE

SERVES 8

110g freshly made white breadcrumbs
1 large onion
15–18 whole cloves or whole nutmeg
1 bay leaf
8 black peppercorns
570ml Channel Island or whole milk
50g butter
2 tablespoons double cream
seasoning

Cut the onion in half and stick the cloves in it (how many you use is a personal matter – I happen to like a pronounced flavour of cloves). If you don't like them at all, you can use some freshly grated nutmeg instead. Place the onion studded with cloves, plus the bay leaf and the peppercorns, in a saucepan together with the milk. Add some salt, then bring everything up to boiling point. Take off the heat, cover the pan and leave in a warm place for the milk to infuse for 2 hours or more (see 11.45 am).

8.55 am

Lower the oven temperature to 170°C/gas mark 3. *Now take a break!* At this point everything should be under control, so you can take time out of the kitchen to help the kids unwrap their presents, have a coffee or tidy the house. After that, prepare and set the lunch table, making sure you have all the right glasses for pre-lunch drinks as well as the table. It's a good idea to arrange the coffee tray now, too, and line up the brandy and liqueur glasses. Pop the plates and serving dishes into the warming oven, and don't forget to warm a large plate for the turkey.

11.45 am

Now is the time to finish off the Bread Sauce. Remove the onion, bay leaf and peppercorns, and keep the onion on one side. Stir the breadcrumbs into the milk and add half of the butter. Leave the saucepan on a very low heat, stirring now and then, until the crumbs have swollen and thickened the sauce – approximately 15 minutes. Now replace the clove-studded onion and again leave the pan in a warm place till the sauce is needed. Just before serving, remove the onion and spices and squeeze it between two saucers to extract all the juice. Reheat gently, then beat the cream and taste to check the seasoning. Pour into a warm serving jug and dot the remaining butter on top and keep warm until needed. Then stir in the butter before serving.

12.00 noon

Fill a saucepan quite full with boiling water, put it on the heat and, when it comes back to the boil, place a steamer on top of the pan and turn it down to a gentle simmer. Put the Christmas pudding in the steamer, cover and leave to steam away until 2.15 pm. You'll need to check the water from time to time and maybe top it up a bit.

12.15 pm

The Christmas pudding brings us, naturally enough, to the Rum Sauce, whose time has now come. Make it as follows:

CHRISTMAS RUM SAUCE

SERVES 8

75g butter
60g plain flour
570ml Channel Island or whole milk
50g caster sugar
4–5 tablespoons dark rum (or more)
1 tablespoon double cream

Place 60g of the butter in a saucepan with 60g flour, pour in the milk, then, using a balloon whisk, whisk everything vigorously together over a medium heat. As soon as it comes to simmering point and has thickened, turn the heat right down to its lowest setting, stir in the sugar and let the sauce cook for 10 minutes. After that, add the rum and the cream. Pour the hot sauce into a jug and dot the remaining butter over the top of the hot sauce, then cover the surface with clingfilm and keep warm until required and whisk before serving.

12.30 pm

Increase the oven temperature to 200°C/gas mark 6. Now get some help, because you've got to lift the turkey out of the oven and it's heavy! Remove the foil from the top and sides of the bird and take off the bacon slices. Now baste the turkey very thoroughly with a long-handled spoon, then return it to the oven for a further 30-45 minutes to finish browning - give it as much basting as you can during this final cooking period. The bacon rashers can be placed on a heatproof plate and put back in the oven for 15-20 minutes to finish cooking till all the fat has melted and there are just very crisp bits left. (I like to serve these crunchy bits with the turkey instead of bacon rolls.)

12.45 pm

After you've dealt with the turkey, parboil the potatoes for 10 minutes, then drain them. Put the lid back on, and shake the potatoes quite heftily in the saucepan so that they become fluffy round the edges. Now take a solid roasting tin, add 50g lard or goose fat to it and place on direct heat to let the fat melt and begin to sizzle. When it is really hot, add the potatoes and (using an oven glove to protect your hands) tip the tin and baste the potatoes so all are coated with fat. Then place the roasting tin in the oven with the turkey.

1.00 pm

Now for the parsnips. If you are not doing Parsnips with Parmesan (see page 193) then parboil them for 10 minutes. Take another roasting tray and add 3 tablespoons of oil and 1 tablespoon of butter to it and place over direct heat. When the butter and oil are hot, add the parsnips and baste them in the same way as the potatoes. By now it will be time for the turkey to come out of the oven.

1.15 pm

Remove the turkey from the oven (see page 263 for how to check the turkey is cooked) and increase the temperature to 230°C/gas mark 8. Place the parsnips on the middle shelf of the oven (with the potatoes on the top) and the chipolatas and bacon rolls on the lowest shelf or floor of the oven.

Transfer the turkey to a warm serving plate: it will be fine left to rest in the kitchen temperature for up to 50 minutes, loosely covered with double foil, without losing its heat. Next pour the giblet stock into a pan and allow it to heat up gently. Tip the turkey fat from the foil into the tin, discard the foil, then spoon off all the excess fat from the roasting tin into a bowl. This fat is *precious*: it's wonderful for sautéing potatoes, and have you ever tried turkey jelly and dripping spread on hot slices of toast and sprinkled with salt and pepper? A wonderful Boxing Day breakfast treat (see page 273)!

Next make the giblet gravy. When you have spooned off the excess fat and juices from the roasting tin and only the 2-3 tablespoons of fat are left, work about 2 level tablespoons flour into this (scraping all the residue from the base and sides of the tin) over a low heat. Now, using a balloon whisk, whisk in the giblet stock, bit by bit, until you have a smooth gravy. Let it bubble and reduce a little to concentrate the flavour, and taste and season. Then pour into a warmed jug and keep warm.

1.30 pm

Turn the chipolatas and bacon rolls over, then you are free for a few minutes to go and have a pre-lunch glass of champagne. You deserve it.

1.45 pm

Now cook the sprouts in a steamer (or just cover them with boiling water), add salt and cook for 5-6 minutes, then drain in a colander. While the sprouts are cooking, summon the carver and get all hands on deck to help dish up. And don't forget that lovely stuffing inside the turkey!

2 pm

Lunch is served. *Bon appétit!*

a little later

Remove the pudding from the steamer and take off the wrapping. Slide a palette knife all round the pudding, then turn it out on to a warmed plate. Place a suitably sized sprig of holly on top. Now warm a ladleful of brandy over direct heat and, as soon as the brandy is hot, turn out the flame and ask someone to set light to it using a long match. Place the ladle, now gently flaming, on top of the pudding - but don't pour it over until you reach the table. (If you don't have a gas hob, warm the brandy in a small saucepan.) When you do, pour it slowly over the pudding, sides and all, and watch it flame to the cheers of the assembled company! When both flames and cheers have died down, serve the pudding with Christmas Rum Sauce (page 267), or Cumberland Rum or Brandy Butter (see page 79).

A VERY IMPORTANT MESSAGE FOR ALL FRAZZLED CHRISTMAS COOKS

The good news is that what you now have, in addition to your aching limbs and heavy eyelids, is a house full of food and absolutely no more cooking to do. So stretch out, fill your glass and *have a very Happy Christmas*!

WHAT'S LEFT?

IF, AFTER WORKING HARD all the year round, you are the one who has to organise, shop and cook for Christmas, there is one big bonus in store for you. It's that, after the big day, there will be a house full of food and, with any luck, you may not have to set foot in a shop till after the New Year. Here are lots of ideas on how to enjoy what's left happily and without too much effort.

TURKEY SOUP
SERVES 6

This is the very last bit of Christmas – warm, comforting bowls of steamy soup as January begins.

FOR THE STOCK

1 turkey carcass (including the skin and any debris, like bits of stuffing)

1 large carrot, peeled and split lengthways

1 onion, peeled and cut in half

2 celery sticks, cut into chunks

2 sprigs thyme

2 bay leaves

12 black peppercorns

a little salt

FOR THE SOUP

900g vegetables (any combination of carrots, leeks, celery and onions)

1 heaped dessertspoon turkey dripping or butter

seasoning

To make the stock, take your largest cooking pot and break the turkey carcass into it (along with all the bits that cling to it), then add the rest of the ingredients and cover with cold water (about 6–7 litres). Bring up to simmering point, skim off any scum that rises to the surface, then simmer the stock for 2 hours. After that strain the stock through a colander and discard the debris. Then strain through a sieve into a large clean pan, bring up to simmering point and let it bubble and reduce down to 1 litre.

Meanwhile, peel and chop the vegetables. Then heat the dripping or butter in a large pan, then add the chopped vegetables, cover and reduce the heat to low and leave them to sweat for 10 minutes. Then add the litre of reduced turkey stock and leave to simmer again with the lid on very gently for 1½ hours. After that purée the soup in a food processor or liquidiser or with a stick blender. Taste to check the seasoning and reheat before serving.

Ladle into warm bowls, freshly baked Irish Soda Bread (overleaf) would be a splendid accompaniment.

< TURKEY DRIPPING ON TOAST

A once-a-year breakfast treat for those who are up and about on Boxing Day and all the other days: very crisp toast spread with turkey dripping (instead of butter), then topped with turkey jelly and lots of freshly milled black pepper and crushed sea salt.

IRISH SODA BREAD

MAKES 1 LOAF, TO SERVE 4-6

Perfect with smoked salmon over Christmas, or hunks of leftover cheese and the previous recipe for turkey soup.

275g wholemeal flour

75g plain flour, plus a little extra for dusting

50g pinhead oatmeal

1 teaspoon bicarbonate of soda

1½ teaspoons salt

1 teaspoon sugar

1 egg

1 x 284ml carton buttermilk

a little milk

1 tablespoon rolled oats, for sprinkling

A baking tray, well greased.

Preheat the oven to 190°C/gas mark 5.

This could not be easier. Begin by placing the dry ingredients in a large, roomy bowl, mix to combine, then beat the egg and buttermilk together, then add them to the bowl too. Start mixing, first with a fork then finish off with your hands, to form a smooth dough. All you do now is shape the dough into an oval 30cm long, adding a dusting of flour if needed, then brush with milk and sprinkle with oats. Now use the blunt side of a knife to make 6-7 diagonal indentations evenly spaced across the top of the bread.

Bake in the centre of the oven for 50-60 minutes, then turn it straight out on to a wire rack to cool. This has a wonderful crust when eaten fresh, but the next day it stays beautifully moist and makes excellent toast.

TURKEY FLAN WITH LEEKS & CHEESE
SERVES 6-8

One thing I know now, being older, is that I would not be making pastry on the days following Christmas. That said, this leftover recipe is too good not to include, so my advice would be to either buy the pastry or make it before Christmas, line the tin with it and freeze it in the tin. As I've now discovered, cooking a flan in a frozen pastry case gives a crisper finish. Alternatively you could buy two ready-prepared fresh pastry cases, freeze them and the filling below will be the right amount.

a 25cm quiche or flan tin lined with 300g shortcrust pastry, frozen

FOR THE FILLING

275-350g cooked turkey, chicken or ham (or a mixture), thinly sliced and cut into roughly 5cm pieces

450g leeks, washed thoroughly and sliced

75g cheese, grated (any kind, or a mixture)

1 egg, beaten

25g freshly grated Parmesan

40g butter, plus extra 1 teaspoon

425ml milk

25g plain flour

whole nutmeg, for grating

cayenne pepper

seasoning

Preheat the oven to 200°C/gas mark 6 and pop in a heavy baking sheet to preheat.

First melt a teaspoon of butter in a frying pan, swirl it round the pan and then, keeping the heat lowish, add the leeks and some salt, cover and let them gently cook for 10-15 minutes and exude some of their juice. After that place the leeks in a sieve, strain off any juices into a bowl and set aside.

While that's happening put the 40g butter, milk and flour in a saucepan and bring up to the boil, whisking all the time, until you have a smooth, thick sauce. Season with salt, pepper and a little nutmeg, then leave the sauce to simmer gently for 5 minutes. Now arrange the leeks over the pastry base, followed by the slices of turkey, chicken or ham.

Then pour the reserved leek juice into the sauce, add the grated cheese and the beaten egg and mix well. Pour the sauce evenly over the contents of the flan and sprinkle the Parmesan on top, together with a dusting of cayenne. Place the flan on the baking sheet on the centre shelf of the oven, then reduce the heat to 180°C/gas mark 4 and bake it for 35-40 minutes.

TURKEY & HAM BENEDICT
SERVES 2 FOR LUNCH OR 4 FOR A SNACK

Can this still be one of the world's great open sandwiches without the eggs? Why not? It doesn't use the classic hollandaise, but an easier version borrowed from *How to Cheat*.

FOR THE OPEN SANDWICHES

2 square ciabatta rolls (approximately 9.5cm square)

10g butter

75g hand-sliced cooked turkey

75g hand-sliced cooked ham

4 cornichons, roughly chopped

25g freshly grated Parmesan

FOR THE NO-PANIC HOLLANDAISE

3 rounded tablespoons crème fraîche

1 teaspoon cornflour

2 egg yolks

¾ tablespoon white wine vinegar

1 dessertspoon lemon juice

50g softened butter

seasoning

TO SERVE

50–75g watercress, any thicker stalks removed

extra virgin olive oil

lemon juice

salt flakes

Preheat the grill to its highest setting for a minimum of 10 minutes.

First make the sauce: spoon the crème fraîche into a small saucepan, then add the cornflour, egg yolks, white wine vinegar and lemon juice. Whisk them all together with a mini-whisk, then over a medium heat, bring the whole lot up to simmering point, whisking continuously until the sauce has thickened. Now remove the sauce from the heat, taste and add some seasoning and a bit more vinegar or lemon if it needs it.

Now split each of the ciabatta rolls in half, toast them on both sides and butter the cut sides. If the rounded sides of the rolls wobble a bit, slice a little off the bottom with a serrated knife to make them sit better. Cut the sliced turkey and ham into roughly 3cm pieces and arrange these, along with the cornichons, on top of the rolls.

Next put the sauce back on the heat and whisk for about 30 seconds, then remove it and whisk in the butter and spoon the sauce over the turkey and ham. Next sprinkle each open sandwich evenly with the Parmesan and pop them under the grill for 3–4 minutes, until bubbling and golden.

Meanwhile toss the watercress with some olive oil and lemon juice and divide between the serving plates, sprinkled with some salt flakes, and serve the grilled sandwiches alongside.

STILTON RAREBIT
SERVES 4 AS A SNACK OR 8 AS A PRE-DINNER NIBBLE

This recipe makes the most of leftover Stilton – but it could be made with any hard cheese (or even a mixture of all those end bits clinging to the rind).

225g Stilton, rind removed

1 egg, beaten

1 large shallot, finely chopped

1 teaspoon Worcestershire sauce

¼ teaspoon English mustard powder

1 heaped teaspoon chopped sage

25g walnut pieces

4 thick slices of bread (or 16 slices of ciabatta 1cm thick), well toasted

1 teaspoon cayenne pepper

Preheat the grill to its highest setting for a minimum of 10 minutes.

First of all line either the grill pan or a baking tray with foil then put the cheese into a mixing bowl. Use a fork to finely crumble the cheese, then stir in the egg, shallot, Worcestershire sauce, mustard, sage and walnuts.

Now spread the cheese mixture thickly over the toast, making sure you take the mixture to the edge or they will burn. Sprinkle with cayenne pepper. Then place them on to the foil-lined grill pan or baking tray and grill for 2 minutes, until the cheese is golden and bubbling. Serve warm. Watercress salad (see page 277) would be a good addition.

SMOKED SALMON OR KIPPER RAREBIT
SERVES 2 FOR LUNCH OR 4 AS A SNACK

If, like us, you order a side of smoked salmon for Christmas, all the trimmings can be used in this. However, this is also good made with kipper fillets (perhaps tucked away in the freezer?). Either way, you can also be using up leftover cheese from Christmas for this loveliest of snack dishes.

approx. 200g smoked kipper fillet
(or slightly less of smoked
salmon)
150ml milk
1 small garlic clove
2 pinches of ground mace
cayenne pepper
1 dessertspoon butter
1 dessertspoon flour
2 hard-boiled eggs (see page 89),
peeled and roughly chopped
1 dessertspoon chopped parsley
100g grated hard cheese such as
Cheddar, Lancashire or Gruyère
2 square ciabatta rolls (approximately
9.5cm square), halved, or 4 thick
slices of bread from a small loaf

A small baking sheet.

Begin by placing the kipper fillet (straight from frozen) in a smallish saucepan with the milk, garlic, mace and two pinches of cayenne. Bring it up to simmering point and poach for about 15 minutes (if you're using chilled smoked kipper, cut the time to 5 minutes). After that, strain off the milk into a bowl and leave the kipper to cool a bit. (For smoked salmon rarebit, warm the milk to infuse it with the garlic and spices first, then continue with the sauce in the same way.)

Make the sauce by melting the butter in a small saucepan, then stir in the flour till smooth and gradually add the milk – switch to a whisk and continue to whisk until all the milk is in and the sauce bubbles and thickens. Leave it on the lowest heat for 3 minutes. Meanwhile, preheat the grill to its highest setting.

Remove the skin from the kipper and break the fish into small flakes (or roughly chop the salmon), then add these to the sauce, along with the chopped eggs and parsley, tasting to check the seasoning. After that, toast the bread on both sides and arrange on a baking sheet (if the rounded sides of the rolls wobble a bit, slice a little off the bottom with a serrated knife to make them sit better).

Finally, spoon out the filling on to each roll or slice of toast, then scatter the grated cheese on top. Give a final dusting of cayenne and place them under the hot grill, about 14cm from the heat source, and cook for 4–5 minutes, until the cheese is melting, bubbling and brown on top.

POTTED ROQUEFORT WITH ARMAGNAC
SERVES 3–4

The thing here is, would you actually have any Roquefort left over? If so, this would make it go even further, but that said it is worth buying some just for this recipe – it may seem unlikely, but it is amazingly good.

100g Roquefort
25g unsalted butter
1 teaspoon Armagnac
a pinch of cayenne pepper

A 150ml bowl or pot.

All you do is mash the Roquefort in a small mixing bowl with a fork – not absolutely smooth. Then add the remaining ingredients and mash again until evenly blended. Spoon into a pot and smooth the surface with the back of a spoon, cover and chill for at least 2 hours. It's great with hot buttered toast and equally good melted over steaks just before serving.

LEEK, POTATO & CHEESE SOUFFLÉ
SERVES 2

It may be hard to believe, but this one is good for using up leftovers – any combination of bits of cheese that lurk unused in dark corners of the fridge and leftover boiled potatoes (always a menace sitting in the fridge and not being used). However, if you don't have any left over, boiling some specially will be well worth it. This will make a very fine supper dish for two vegetarians or for those who often give meat a skip. The potatoes give the soufflé a lovely crusty top with a squidgy inside. A salad with a lemon dressing would be a good accompaniment and a dollop of chutney on the side wouldn't go amiss.

50g leek, halved, washed and thinly
    sliced
110g boiled potatoes
50g strong Cheddar, grated
    (1 tablespoon reserved for topping)
25g butter
4 tablespoons soured cream
4 tablespoons natural yoghurt
2 eggs, separated
salt
cayenne pepper
whole nutmeg, for grating
FOR THE TOPPING
the reserved Cheddar (see above)
1 dessertspoon freshly grated
    Parmesan
cayenne pepper

A soufflé dish with a base
    measurement of 13cm, 7cm
    deep, well buttered and a
    small baking tray.

Preheat the oven to 200°C/gas mark 6.

Begin by heating the butter in a small saucepan, then stir in the sliced leek and cook gently for 5 minutes. Then add the soured cream and yoghurt, give it all a good stir and cook on a very low heat for a further 5 minutes or so to soften the leek and flavour the sauce. Then take the pan off the heat and let it cool for 5 minutes.

Now beat the yolks into the cooled sauce, and grate the potatoes straight into the pan and beat into the sauce. Lastly, beat in all but 1 tablespoon of the grated Cheddar. Season with a little salt, cayenne and nutmeg, then transfer to a large bowl. In a separate (grease-free) bowl, whisk the egg whites until stiff and stir 1 heaped tablespoon into the cheese mixture to slacken it and make it easier to fold in the rest. Taste for seasoning before carefully folding in the remaining egg whites.

Pour the whole lot into the soufflé dish and sprinkle the top with the reserved Cheddar, Parmesan and a sprinkling of cayenne. Place on a baking tray and bake on the centre shelf of the oven for 25 minutes, or until well risen and golden brown. Serve as soon as possible (it will shrink a bit on the way to the table), but even when it is shrunken and cold it still tastes good!

ENGLISH COLONIAL CURRY WITH TURKEY
SERVES 4

There is something about an uncomplicated, old-fashioned curry-powder curry after all the Christmas feasting. Its sheer simplicity offers a much-needed change of gear. It is also equally good made with leftover chicken or beef.

600g cooked turkey, chopped into chunks
1 tablespoon turkey dripping
1 large onion, finely chopped
2 sticks of celery, chopped
1 clove garlic, crushed
1 heaped tablespoon plain flour
1 teaspoon turmeric
1 teaspoon ground ginger
1 heaped tablespoon Sharwood's Hot Curry Powder (for Madras)
725ml hot stock (made with Marigold bouillon)
1 medium dessert or Bramley apple, cored and chopped (no need to peel)
25g sultanas
1 heaped tablespoon mango chutney
2 tablespoons grated creamed coconut
a squeeze of lemon
seasoning

Heat the dripping and fry the onion and celery over a medium heat, tossing them around till softened and well browned at the edges, then add the garlic and toss that around for a minute. Now stir in the flour, turmeric, ginger and curry powder to soak up all the juices, and after that gradually stir in the stock. When the sauce begins to bubble add the apple, sultanas, mango chutney and grated coconut, plus some seasoning.

Turn the heat down to a gentle simmer and let it cook for 30 minutes. After that, add the turkey pieces and a squeeze of lemon juice, stir well, put a lid on and simmer gently for a further 10 minutes to reheat the turkey. Serve with basmati rice, poppadoms, mango chutney and lime pickle.

MINCEMEAT & APPLE CRUMBLE FLAN WITH ALMONDS
SERVES 6

If you've got leftover mincemeat this will cheer up a January Sunday lunch beautifully. A ready-made pastry flan case will also save you time, which we have discovered works really well when frozen first.

400g mincemeat (approx.)

110g Cox's apples, cored (no need to peel)

110g Bramley apples, cored (no need to peel)

1 x 230g fresh pastry flan case (frozen)

a little melted butter

1 tablespoon brandy

1 rounded teaspoon semolina

icing sugar, for dusting

FOR THE CRUMBLE

20g chilled butter, cut into small dice

40g self-raising flour

25g demerara sugar

½ teaspoon ground cinnamon

25g whole almonds (skin on is OK)

A heated baking sheet.

Preheat the oven to 200°C/gas mark 6.

First, make the crumble. All you do is place the butter, flour, sugar and cinnamon in a processor and give things a whiz until the mixture resembles crumbs. Then add the almonds and process again – not too fast – until they are fairly finely chopped but with a few chunky bits left. If you don't have a processor, in a large bowl rub the butter into the sifted flour until it resembles crumbs, then stir in the sugar, cinnamon and almonds (which you can chop by hand).

Now chop the apples into small pieces – a mini chopper will make light work of this. Then mix them in with the mincemeat in a bowl, along with the brandy. Then brush the inside of the pastry case with a little melted butter and sprinkle the semolina evenly over the base. Place on the hot baking sheet and spoon in the apple mixture, pressing it down well. Then, simply sprinkle the crumble all over the apple mixture. Using the flat of your hands, press it down quite firmly; the more tightly it is packed together, the crisper it will be.

Put the tart on the centre shelf of the oven, reduce the temperature down to 190°C/gas mark 5 and bake for 40 minutes, by which time the apples will be soft and the topping golden brown and crisp. Leave it to rest for 10–15 minutes before serving dusted with icing sugar.

HOGMANAY

OR NEW YEAR'S EVE to us southerners, and the feast that ends the feasting of the past few days. It seems entirely fitting to have a flavour of Scotland and, if you're not out partying, why not invite friends round to supper and end the year on a peaceful note? When the clock strikes midnight it is traditional for us to take a glass of some smoky, peaty single malt. So to all those cooks who have generously cooked their way through Christmas for their friends and family, cheers, and we hope the new year will be a really good one!

SOUFFLÉD ARBROATH SMOKIE CREAMS
with Foaming Hollandaise
SERVES 8 AS A STARTER

This is an old favourite that never fails to delight. It's easy, can be prepared in advance and fulfils all the criteria of a really top-notch first course. Remember to start the fish the night before and, if you can't get smokies, good-quality finnan haddock will do well.

1 pair Arbroath smokies (about 400g)
   or 225–275g smoked haddock
2 eggs, lightly beaten
275ml double cream
225–300g sliced smoked salmon
whole nutmeg, for grating
seasoning
some watercress, to serve

Eight 7.5cm ramekins, 4cm deep, well
   buttered, and a large roasting tin.

Begin by carefully skinning and boning the Arbroath smokies – you'll find the flesh will part very easily from the bones. (You should end up with about 225–275g of flesh after this.) Flake the fish and place it in a blender, or food processor, along with some seasoning and a good grating of nutmeg. Blend until the fish has turned to a smooth, even pulp, then blend in the lightly beaten eggs. Transfer it to a bowl, cover and leave in the fridge overnight.

Next day, to prepare ahead, line the base and sides of each ramekin with smoked salmon – don't worry that you're doing this in pieces and patches as it won't show when they're finally turned out. Then return the fish mixture to the blender or processor together with the cream and blend them thoroughly together. Then divide the fish mixture equally between the ramekins, cover and chill till needed.

When you're ready to cook, preheat the oven to 190°C/gas mark 5 and place the roasting tin filled with about 2.5cm of boiling water on the centre shelf of the oven. Place the ramekins in the roasting tin, then cook for exactly 40 minutes.

To serve, have some warmed plates ready then turn out each soufflé, holding the ramekin with a cloth and tipping it out quickly upside-down onto your hand and just as quickly flip it over on to the plate. Garnish with watercress and pour the hollandaise over each one.

FOAMING HOLLANDAISE

2 eggs, separated
1 dessertspoon lemon juice
1 dessertspoon white wine vinegar
110g butter
seasoning

Begin by placing the egg yolks in a small bowl and season them. Then place them in a food processor or blender and blend them thoroughly for about 1 minute. After that, heat the lemon juice and white wine vinegar in a small saucepan until the mixture starts to bubble and simmer. Switch the processor or blender on again and pour the hot liquid on to the egg yolks in a slow, steady stream. After that, switch off. Now, using the same saucepan, melt the butter over a gentle heat, being very careful not to let it brown. When the butter is foaming, switch the processor or blender on once more and pour in the butter in a thin, slow, steady trickle; the slower you add it the better. (If it helps you to use a jug and not pour from the saucepan, warm a jug with boiling water, discard the boiling water and then pour the butter mixture into that first.) When all the butter has been incorporated, wipe around the sides of the processor bowl or blender with a spatula to incorporate all the sauce, then give the sauce one more quick burst and you should end up with a lovely smooth, thick, buttery sauce. Now whisk the remaining two egg whites to soft peaks in a large, clean mixing bowl and fold into the sauce immediately.

NOTE Foaming Hollandaise can be made well ahead and gently re-heated. It also freezes well.

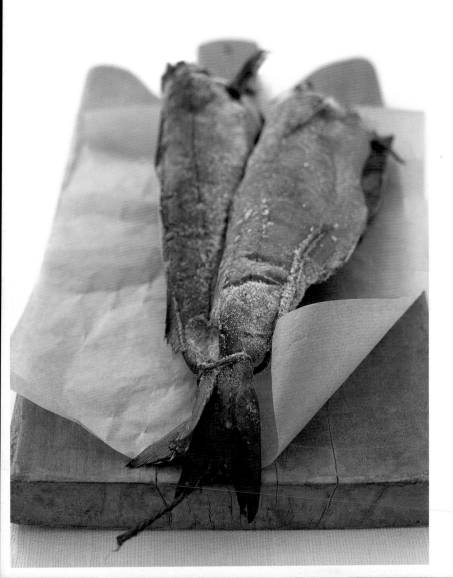

PARTAN BREE (FRESH CRAB SOUP)
SERVES 6

This beautiful Scottish recipe makes an excellent first course for Hogmanay. For those Scots in exile, Cornish hand-picked crabmeat fits the bill.

200–250g mixed white and brown crabmeat (or 1 x 100g tub hand-picked white Cornish crab and 1 x 100g tub hand-picked brown Cornish crab)
570ml whole milk
570ml vegetable stock (made with Marigold bouillon)
75g long grain rice
1½ teaspoons anchovy paste
½ teaspoon ground mace
¼ teaspoon cayenne pepper
150ml single cream
6 tablespoons fresh lemon juice
seasoning

Heat together the milk, stock and rice in a medium-sized saucepan until it reaches simmering point. Stir well, put a lid on and cook the rice gently for 15 minutes. Then remove it from the heat and add the brown crab meat, anchovy paste, mace and cayenne pepper and use a stick blender or liquidiser to blend the soup until smooth.

Then return it to the saucepan if in a liquidiser and stir in the white crabmeat and single cream, adding a little seasoning and a bit more cayenne if it needs it. Heat the soup gently without letting it boil, then stir in the lemon juice and check the seasoning again just before you serve it in warmed bowls. If you want to make this in advance, after blending let it get quite cold and store in the fridge, then continue as above.

HAGGIS PIE WITH TATTIES & NEEPS & WHISKY SAUCE
SERVES 6-8

This way of serving haggis is perfect for a New Year's supper party, as it can be prepared well ahead and cooked when you need it. Serve it with any simple green vegetable.

900g haggis (that is 2 x 450g)
600g swede, cut into 4cm chunks
80g butter
1.15kg Desiree potatoes
50g mature Cheddar, coarsely grated
FOR THE SAUCE
1 tablespoon groundnut oil
25g butter
700g onions, peeled and sliced
1 rounded tablespoon flour
200ml whisky
1 tablespoon Worcestershire sauce
1 teaspoon English mustard powder
725ml vegetable stock (made with
    Marigold bouillon)
seasoning

A 20 x 28 x 5cm baking dish, buttered.

You will need to cook the haggis first so place them both in a fan (or conventional) steamer and steam for 1 hour exactly, then leave them to cool. Meanwhile, place the pieces of swede in a saucepan with some salt and enough boiling water to just cover, then simmer gently for about 15 minutes, or until they are tender but not mushy. Then drain and chop them with the pulse button in a food processor (or with a sharp knife), adding a knob of the butter until they are finely chopped, then season.

Now peel the potatoes and cut them into even-sized pieces, then steam them (adding salt) for about 25 minutes, until they're completely tender. Drain off the water, return the potatoes to the saucepan and cover them with a clean tea towel for about 5 minutes to absorb the steam. Next add the remaining butter and mash them to a purée – the best way to do this is with an electric hand whisk. Season if needed.

If the pie is not going to be eaten straight away make sure all the layers are cool before putting them in a pie dish. First slit open the haggis casing and spread the contents out evenly over the base of the dish, then the chopped swede and finally a layer of mashed potatoes. Use a palette knife to smooth the top and if you like make a ridged pattern on the surface before sprinkling the cheese all over. Now cover with clingfilm and keep chilled in the fridge until you need it.

You can make the sauce ahead as well. Heat the groundnut oil and butter in a large saucepan, then add the onions and let them cook very gently for 45 minutes, until they have become mellow and caramelised. Then stir in the flour and add 150ml of the whisky, the Worcestershire sauce, mustard and hot stock (whisking all the time). Taste and season and continue to simmer gently for 20 minutes. After that, cool and refrigerate until needed.

To cook the pie, first preheat the oven to 200°C/gas mark 6, then place the pie on a baking tray in the centre of the oven for 45–50 minutes, until the top is crusty and golden. Heat the sauce with the remaining whisky and spoon a little over each portion, with the rest handed round.

BRAISED VENISON WITH BACON, CHESTNUTS & WILD MUSHROOMS IN A RICH MADEIRA SAUCE

SERVES 6

This casserole freezes extremely well and fits the bill perfectly for New Year. Because it's braised slowly, there are lots of lovely flavours and because the sauce, made with rich Madeira, is dark and glossy, this cries out for a pile of creamy, fluffy mashed potato.

900g cubed shoulder of venison

250g bacon lardons or cubetti di pancetta

200g frozen peeled chestnuts, defrosted (or vac-packed)

20g dried porcini mushrooms

570ml Madeira

2 tablespoons olive oil

2 medium onions, sliced

2 cloves garlic, sliced

175g small dark-gilled chestnut mushrooms

1 rounded tablespoon plain flour

a few sprigs of thyme

2 bay leaves

seasoning

A 3.5 litre lidded flameproof casserole.

Preheat the oven to 140°C/gas mark 1.

Begin this by heating half the oil in the casserole and, when it's hot, add the onions and cook them for about 6 minutes, till they're dark and caramelised at the edges. Then add the garlic, stir and cook for a further minute before removing the whole lot to a plate, using a draining spoon.

Next, add the bacon lardons to the casserole, toss them around in the hot fat till they turn golden, then transfer them to the plate.

Now add the rest of the oil and, keeping the heat high, brown the cubes of meat, about six at a time, removing them to join the onions as you go. After that, add the fresh mushrooms and toss them around in the hot juices for another minute, then return everything from the plate back to the casserole.

Stir well now, add some seasoning, then sprinkle in the flour, stirring again to soak up the juices, then gradually add the Madeira, still stirring. Finally, add the thyme, the bay leaves and the dried porcini (having rinsed them first under a tap and broken up any extra-large pieces).

As soon as the whole thing reaches simmering point, put a lid on and transfer the casserole to the oven to braise slowly for 2 hours. Then add the chestnuts and cook for 30 minutes more.

NOTE This also works a treat with beef.

CRANACHAN WITH CARAMELISED OATMEAL & RASPBERRY SAUCE
SERVES 8

One of my own favourite Scottish desserts. In *The Summer Collection* we made Caledonian ice cream with caramelised oatmeal and now we've discovered it works really well with Cranachan. We find that frozen Scottish (or British) raspberries work better than the expensive imported fresh ones at Christmas.

50g caster sugar, plus 3 heaped
    tablespoons
2 tablespoons water
125g pinhead oatmeal
450g raspberries, frozen
3 tablespoons whisky
1½ teaspoons pure vanilla extract
450ml whipping cream

A small baking sheet, lightly oiled, and
    six sturdy conical (or other)
    275ml serving glasses.

To make the caramelised oatmeal, put 50g caster sugar and 2 tablespoons of water in a small saucepan over a low heat and leave it for 5 minutes. Then take a medium-sized frying pan. Place it on a medium heat and, when the pan is hot, add the oatmeal and swirl it round in the pan constantly so it browns evenly – which it will do in 5 minutes. Then quickly remove the oatmeal to a glass heatproof jug to prevent it becoming too brown. By now the sugar crystals in the pan will have dissolved, so you can turn the heat right up and let it boil (watching it like a hawk) until it begins to turn a rich caramel colour, rather like dark runny honey.

As soon as it reaches that stage, stir in the toasted oatmeal, remove it from the heat and quickly pour the mixture on to the oiled baking sheet then leave it on one side to get cool and firm (which will take approximately 15 minutes). Now break it up into small pieces then crush it in a processor until the tiny pinhead oats have become separate again.

Next deal with the raspberries by putting them (still frozen) into a medium saucepan with the remaining caster sugar and heat until the raspberries start to defrost and collapse. Bring them up to a gentle simmer and cook them for about 5 minutes, then cool and whiz them to a purée in a processor and finally push through a nylon sieve to extract the pips.

Now add the whisky and vanilla to the cream and whip it to the floppy stage. Reserve 2 tablespoons of the caramelised oatmeal for garnish, then fold in the rest into the whipped cream. Put a heaped tablespoonful of cream in each glass, then a couple of tablespoonfuls of purée and repeat, finishing with the cream. Lastly sprinkle on the reserved oatmeal. Cover and chill in the fridge till needed.

SCOTS TRIFLE WITH DRAMBUIE
SERVES 6-8

This is my take on a traditional Scottish favourite. Great for a Hogmanay celebration and a rich, luscious ending to the Christmas holiday before the frugality of January sets in. I'm ashamed to say we once ate all of it between four!

6 trifle sponges
3 heaped tablespoons marmalade
1 large navel orange, zest and juice
75ml Drambuie
75g ratafia biscuits (or amaretti)
FOR THE CUSTARD
600ml double cream
6 egg yolks
1 dessertspoon cornflour
50g caster sugar
FOR THE TOPPING
300ml double cream
75ml Drambuie
9 ratafia biscuits (or 4 amaretti)
20g toasted flaked almonds

A 1.5 litre glass bowl.

First of all, split the trifle sponges in half lengthways, spread one half of each sponge with marmalade and form them back into sandwiches. Cut each one across into three and arrange the pieces, cut-side uppermost, in the base of the glass bowl.

Next mix the orange juice, orange zest and Drambuie together and carefully pour it all over the sponges, then set aside for about 20 minutes for the sponges to soak it all up (tilting the bowl a couple of times to encourage this). Meanwhile, to make the custard: heat the cream in a medium saucepan over a gentle heat to just below simmering point. Meanwhile, whisk the egg yolks, cornflour and sugar together in a medium bowl, using a balloon whisk. Next, whisking the egg mixture all the time, gradually pour the hot cream into the bowl.

When it is all in, immediately return the whole lot back to the saucepan using a rubber spatula. Now back it goes on to the same gentle heat as you continue to whisk until the custard is thick and smooth, which will happen as soon as it reaches simmering point (don't worry, it won't curdle – if it does look at all grainy, it will become smooth again when whisked off the heat). Allow it to cool.

Now sprinkle the biscuits (slightly broken if you are using amaretti) evenly over the trifle sponges and after that pour the cooled custard over them. Next whip together the cream and Drambuie until the cream is firm but still floppy.

Now cover the custard with the whipped cream – the best way to do this is to spoon some of the cream in blobs around the edge first, so that the blobs are touching the side of the bowl, and then gradually fill in more blobs towards the centre. When the custard is completely covered, use the back of a spoon to spread it out evenly. Cover with clingfilm (or an upturned bowl) and chill it in the fridge for at least 2 hours or, better, for longer (even overnight). Before serving, sprinkle with toasted almonds and whole ratafia biscuits or, if you are using amaretti (because they are bigger) break them up a little bit first.

BLACK BUN
SERVES 12

If you would like to entertain some friends on New Year's Eve and include an authentic Hogmanay tradition, Black Bun is a spicy fruit cake served with a glass or two of whisky as the clock chimes midnight ('bun', by the way, is the Scottish term for plum cake). The pastry case was originally bread, which kept the juices and flour from escaping, and was then discarded – pastry now being used to make it more edible. My thanks to Kay Smith up in Terregles in Dumfries, who gave me the recipe.

100ml whisky
75g dark molasses sugar
2 teaspoons ground ginger
½ teaspoon ground cloves
1 teaspoon ground cinnamon
1 teaspoon ground allspice
⅛ teaspoon freshly milled black
    pepper
300g ready-made shortcrust pastry
    (made with butter)
1 small egg, beaten
110g self-raising flour
300g currants
110g muscatel (or any large) raisins
50g whole candied peel, finely chopped
50g almonds (skin on is OK), cut into
    slivers, or toasted flaked almonds

A deep, loose-based 15cm cake tin.

Preheat the oven to 140°C/gas mark 1.

First, put the whisky, sugar and spices into a mixing bowl, give it a quick whisk and leave to one side for the sugar to dissolve while you roll the pastry.

Take one-third of the pastry and roll it to a round about 2mm thick. Then take the loose base from the cake tin, place it on the rolled pastry and cut out a 15cm disc, which will be used for the top. Put it on a tray and cover with a piece of clingfilm while you line the tin.

Now take the remaining pastry, knead it into a round ball. Then roll the pastry to a circle about 31cm in diameter and lift it into the cake tin, then use your fingers to press out any folds in the pastry around the sides of the tin and leave the edges hanging over all round.

Next for the filling – whisk 2 tablespoons of the beaten egg into the whisky mixture and then whisk in the flour until you have a smooth batter. Now stir in the currants, raisins, candied peel and almonds until the fruits are evenly coated with the batter.

Pile the cake mix into the pastry case and even out the top – but don't press it down too much. Now use your fingers and thumbs to press the pastry edges to an even thickness of 2mm, then trim away the edge of the pastry to leave a 3cm border above the line of the cake filling. Now fold the overhanging pastry in over the cake mix, brush with beaten egg and position the prepared pastry disc on top. Press the edges of the pastry down to seal it, then use the prongs of a fork to make a pattern all round the edges.

Now if you like you can roll and cut the trimmings into two strips which can be arranged into a cross on the top like the flag of Scotland. Then take a skewer and make a hole in each quarter of the cake all the way down to the base. When the skewer is touching the base give it a wiggle to widen the hole slightly. Bake the bun in the centre of the oven for 2½ hours. After about 1 hour, check the bun and if it is getting too dark cover it loosely with a piece of baking parchment.

When the cooking time is up the pastry will be a deep golden brown. Leave it to cool completely before removing from the tin, then when it is completely cold wrap it in a piece of foil and store it in a cake tin for at least 3 weeks to mature.

FESTIVE SUGAR PLUMS
MAKES 12

These are great to serve with coffee and drinks after dinner and are so simple – they're literally made in moments.

200g luxury dried fruit
25g ground almonds
2 tablespoons chopped glacé ginger
1 dessertspoon orange juice
the grated zest of 1 medium orange
25g ready-made marzipan
2 tablespoons white caster sugar
1 teaspoon mixed spice
12 pistachio nuts

Put the dried fruit, almonds and ginger in a food processor and chop finely (or chop by hand). Then add the orange juice and zest and whiz briefly again. Now divide both the fruit mixture and the marzipan into 12 pieces and roll into balls.

Then cut the fruit balls in half and sandwich them back together with a marzipan ball in the middle. Next, mix the caster sugar with the mixed spice and roll the balls in the mixture. Finally, cut the pistachios into thin slivers and put them on top of the sugar plums to imitate leaves.

FOR AULD LANG SYNE, MY DEAR,

for auld lang syne

WE'LL TAK' A CUP O' KINDNESS YET,

FOR AULD LANG SYNE

CONVERSION CHART

All these are approximate conversions, which have either been rounded up or down. In a few recipes it has been necessary to modify them very slightly. It's best never to mix metric and imperial measures in one recipe and to stick to one system or the other.

WEIGHTS

10g	½ oz
20	¾
25	1
40	1½
50	2
60	2½
75	3
110	4
125	4½
150	5
175	6
200	7
225	8
250	9
275	10
350	12
450	1lb
700	1lb 8oz
900	2
1.35kg	3

DIMENSIONS

3mm	⅛ inch
5mm	¼
1cm	½
2	¾
2.5	1
3	1¼
4	1½
4.5	1¾
5	2
6	2½
7.5	3
9	3½
10	4
13	5
13.5	5¼
15	6
16	6½
18	7
19	7½
20	8
23	9
24	9½
25.5	10
28	11
30	12

VOLUME

55ml	2fl oz
75	3
150	5 (¼ pint)
275	10 (½ pint)
570	1 pint
725	1¼
1 litre	1¾
1.2	2
1.5	2½
2.25	4

OVEN TEMPERATURES

GAS MARK		
1	140°C	275°F
2	150	300
3	170	325
4	180	350
5	190	375
6	200	400
7	220	425
8	230	450
9	240	475

NOTES ON INGREDIENTS All eggs are large free-range. All meat and poultry is British, and we advise buying free-range wherever possible and fish from sustainable sources.
It should be noted it is recommended that the daily salt intake for adults should not exceed 6g.
SPOONS An important aspect of measurement comes in the shape of spoons. I am afraid I can't accept the official version exemplified by sets. I much prefer to use what was originally intended: real tablespoons, dessertspoons and teaspoons. A useful point to remember is 2 teaspoons equates to 1 dessertspoon, 2 dessertspoons to 1 tablespoon. All spoon measurements are level unless otherwise stated in the recipe.

General information about equipment and ingredients, and a complete list of stockists is available at deliaonline.com

INDEX

ART DIRECTION & DESIGN Vanessa Holden
PHOTOGRAPHY Petrina Tinslay
FOOD STYLING Alison Attenborough
PROPS STYLING Marcus Hay
PROJECT EDITOR Muna Reyal
COPY EDITOR Lesley Levene
FOOD EDITOR Lindsey Greensted-Benech
PERSONAL MANAGER TO DELIA SMITH Melanie Grocott
PRODUCTION Helen Everson

Published in 2009 by Ebury Press, an imprint of Ebury Publishing.
A Random House Group Company

10 9 8 7 6 5 4 3 2 1

Addresses for companies within the Random House Group can be found
at www.randomhouse.co.uk

The Random House Group Limited Reg. No. 954009

A CIP catalogue record for this book is available from the British Library.

The Random House Group Limited supports the Forest Stewardship
Council (FSC), the leading international forest certification organisation.
All our titles that are printed on Greenpeace approved FSC certified paper
carry the FSC logo. Our paper procurement policy can be found at
www.rbooks.co.uk/environment

Colour origination by Alta Image.
Printed and bound by Firmengruppe APPL, aprinta druck, Wemding,
Germany.

To buy books by your favourite authors and register for offers, visit
www.rbooks.co.uk

ISBN 978 0 091 93306 7